System under Stress

Homeland Security and American Politics

Donald F. Kettl
University of Wisconsin–Madison

CQ PRESS

A Division of Congressional Quarterly Inc.
Washington, D.C.

CQ Press
1255 22nd St., N.W., Suite 400
Washington, D.C. 20037

Phone, 202-729-1900
Toll-free, 1-866-4CQ-PRESS (1-866-427-7737)

www.cqpress.com

♾ The paper used in this publication exceeds the requirements of the American National Standard for Information Sciences—Permanence of Paper for Printed Library Materials, ANSI Z39.48-1992.

Cover design: Auburn Associates, Inc.
Composition: BMWW

Photo credits:
AP/Wide World Photos: 5, 16, 48, 115
Reuters: 59, 80, 101

Printed and bound in the United States of America

08   07   06   05   04   5   4   3   2   1

Library of Congress Cataloging-in-Publication Data

Kettl, Donald F.
  System under stress : homeland security and American politics / Donald Kettl.
    p. cm. — (Public affairs and policy administration series)
  Includes bibliographical references and index.
  ISBN 1-56802-888-1 (alk. paper)
  1. United States—Politics and government.   2. Intergovernmental cooperation—United States.   3. National security—United States.   4. Terrorism—United States—Prevention.   5. Civil defense—United States.   6. Public administration—United States.   I. Title: Homeland security and American politics.   II. Title.   III. Series.

JK421.K482 2004
320.973—dc22   2004001913

Contents

Foreword

The September 11, 2001, attacks hit the United States with an awesome force. Americans discovered the power of a small group of determined terrorists to strike a terrible blow, but we also discovered the tremendous heroism of our first responders and the courage of our fellow citizens. If our country learned the costs of such an attack, we learned as well the critical importance of becoming better prepared to prevent others like it in the future. For many Americans, homeland security, which once seemed largely a fiction of the silver screen, now became a necessary—if unwelcome—focus. Public officials in Washington, D.C., and across the country soon found this challenge at the very center of their work, as well.

Learning the lessons of September 11 isn't just a matter of determining what happened and how it might have been prevented, however. That terrible day also teaches important lessons about the strength and vibrancy of American government. It tells us about what is important to government and what makes that government work best. It underlines the critical importance of our shared ideals and the strength of our political institutions. It warns us about what we need to do better and smarter.

As I have testified before members of Congress, this involves not merely a reorganization of government but a transformation of what government does—and how it does it. This transformation will not take place overnight. It will be a long-term effort that requires a close partnership between government and its citizens. It will demand a careful rethinking by citizens about the values inherent in our political system and which of these we most want to protect.

That is why Don Kettl's *System under Stress* is such an important book. It tells the story of what happened and how government responded. But it also asks us to think about what in American life matters most and how best to defend it. These questions lie at the core of government and demand the most thoughtful examination by all citizens. Any individual who cares about America's future must grapple with the questions that Kettl raises in this provocative work.

Dick Thornburgh
Former attorney general of the United States
Former governor of Pennsylvania

Preface

The study of American government often proceeds from the idea that our political system—its institutions, its officials, and even its citizens—behaves in relatively predictable and comprehensible ways. That is what political science is all about: identifying and explaining such patterns and behaviors to make sense of them. No matter how dramatic the ups and downs of an election cycle, no matter how bold a proposal to reinvent government, no matter how innovative a new law or piece of legislation, historically most changes to our political system have fallen within a relatively narrow spectrum. But what happens to that system when a major shock shakes its foundations? What can such a profound upheaval tell us about the system's ability to respond? How does it help define the core truths and enduring principles that lie at the heart of American government? And how can we evaluate the system's response to better understand how it can adapt to the diverse challenges we are likely to face in the future?

On September 11, 2001, terrorists launched a sophisticated series of attacks on the United States. For days, the nation stood paralyzed. Americans for the first time confronted the reality that some individuals so hated this country that they were willing to commit devastating suicide attacks against ordinary citizens. Schools closed for fear of subsequent strikes. Businesses strained to operate amidst the chaos. The skies rang eerily silent, save for the roar of patrolling fighter planes. The stock market, which had weathered countless economic booms and busts, closed for four full days. Television stations broadcast stories of the incredible heroism of New York City's firefighters as well as the terrible failure of the intelligence community to detect the crippling attacks. Members of Congress rallied in an unprecedented show of bipartisanship. President George W. Bush struggled to address the country's need for reassurance and action, and in the process transformed his presidency.

As extraordinary as these responses were, they foreshadowed even deeper changes that would take place across the American political landscape in the following years. No longer could Americans afford to maintain their insular, post–cold war focus on domestic issues. September 11 harshly and vividly showed that political unrest "over there" could spill over into the United States in the form of terrorist activities "right here." Officials and citizens alike debated the role the nation ought to play in the turbulent

vi

twenty-first-century global community. Quite suddenly, Americans found themselves coming to grips with "homeland security" as a new aspect of their everyday lives.

At an institutional level, government officials fought to devise and implement strategies to protect the nation from future attacks. In the frightening event that those attacks should occur, they also worked to ensure that they could provide the most effective response. They strove to improve coordination among the nation's intelligence communities. In the nation's airports and seaports, officials rushed to tighten security. Through the USA Patriot Act, the boundaries of privacy were shifted in the name of security. And a new cabinet department with the directive to oversee it all was created.

This book tells the two central homeland security stories: the terrible impact of the September 11 attacks and the American system's struggle to respond. It weaves together an account of the tragedy with an analysis of how the system reacted—from the frontline heroics of New York firefighters to the political strategies of President Bush and members of Congress. By looking at the issue of homeland security through different levels of analysis—the executive, congressional, and judicial response; the role of federal, state, and local bureaucracies; policymaking; and individuals' civil rights and liberties—this text illustrates chapter by chapter how the system's key players have interacted to help resolve the problems this new era presents.

In the first chapter, I examine the attacks' stunning impact and the immediate response of the nation's leaders. Chapter 2 looks at the breakdowns in the system that allowed the attacks to occur and the efforts by national leaders to plug holes in the coordination of intelligence. In Chapter 3, I explore the broader coordination problems in the federal bureaucracy; Chapter 4 probes how state and local governments became involved in the homeland security strategy. Chapter 5 studies how the political system deals with the policy problem of trying to maximize protection against threats that can never completely be eliminated. In Chapter 6, I ask whether the search for greater security inevitably requires the sacrifice of civil rights and liberties. Chapter 7 concludes the analysis and addresses the central question: How does the American political system respond to such crushing strain?

System under Stress gets at this last question by using homeland security and the events of September 11 as a kind of "stress test." Cardiologists often rely on the stress test, in which a patient exercises on a treadmill and the physician examines how the patient's heart responds, to diagnose how well the heart works and what underlying problems it might have. The cardiologist uses the results of the stress test to prescribe the right cures: more exercise, carefully calibrated medicine, and other changes to help the patient's heart beat better and longer. Likewise, the stress test of the attacks served to diagnose what works well in American government—and what does not.

In the aftermath of the September 11 attacks, the American governmental system is very different, and the pressures that caused these changes are unlikely to ebb any time soon. At the same time, the other big policy issues in American government have not simply evaporated. Strong forces are pushing them back into the debate, and serious backsliding has resulted. On September 12, analysts decreed that "everything has changed." But how much has really changed—and how much have the old and deep-rooted forces in American politics dragged the system back toward where it was before?

Responding to such ordeals will likely be a prime challenge for America's leaders for some time. The issues explored here will set the signposts needed to guide the nation. Given the scope and importance of homeland security, this book ought to be of keen interest to students in a wide variety of courses: American government, public policy and public administration, intergovernmental relations, and focused instruction in homeland security.

ACKNOWLEDGMENTS

In writing this book, I am greatly indebted to the wonderful staff at CQ Press, who provided enthusiastic support and invaluable encouragement along the way. I especially want to thank Brenda Carter and Charisse Kiino for their encouragement of the project; Daphne Levitas for her skilled help with the tables, figures, and photographs; Nancy Geltman for her keen editorial eye in sharpening the prose; and Lorna Notsch for her uncanny instinct for finding even better ways to express what I was trying to say. Elise Frasier was simply indispensable in helping me bring the far-ranging issues together into a tighter argument.

I am also deeply indebted to MaryAnne Borrelli, Connecticut College; Ross Cheit, Brown University; Vincent Moscardelli, University of Massachusetts, Amherst; Ray Owen, University of Pittsburgh; Charles Shipan, University of Iowa; and one other anonymous reviewer. Their comments unquestionably strengthened this book. Kristine Berg provided invaluable research help in sorting through the avalanche of data and documents that have quickly accumulated around the puzzle of homeland security.

In the process of writing the book, I had unexpected personal contact with first responders. I developed a bleeding ulcer—from medication I was taking, not from the stress of writing the book! The wonderful care I received helped get me back on my feet in a few months. I'm especially grateful to the city of Madison's emergency medical technicians, Janice Cooney, Dr. Mark Reichelderfer and his medical team, and Dr. Layton Rikkers and his surgical team. The experience made me even more grateful for my wife, Sue, who was not only a loving companion but also a consummate nurse.

During 2002 and 2003, I worked with the Century Foundation as executive director of their Project on Federalism and Homeland Security. I am grateful to the Century Foundation's president, Richard C. Leone, for his support of this project, and to its vice president, Greg Anrig, for his insight and comments on the manuscript. This book simply would not have been possible if it had not been for the intellectual and financial support of the foundation.

Most of all, I am grateful to the thousands of Americans who work daily in homeland security to help make the nation safer. The book is dedicated to them—and especially to the hundreds of first responders who made the ultimate sacrifice on the morning of September 11.

C h a p t e r

1

Reading the Vital Signs:
The Response to 9/11

WHEN I WAS IN COLLEGE I worked at a string of truly awful summer jobs. At one company a team of us worked to repair frosted glass panels of the kind that cover the recessed fluorescent light fixtures in office buildings. You have undoubtedly seen them—the fluorescent light tubes sit inside a metal case in the ceiling, and a textured glass panel flips up and locks into place to diffuse the light and make the fixture more attractive. Another company had won a contract to build the fixtures we worked on, but when the thousands of glass panels arrived at the construction site, workers discovered that they were a fraction of an inch too wide and could not be locked into place. The glass inside the frame was too large and could not be machined down. So the company contracted with a small business in my hometown to take the panels apart using air-powered screwdrivers, remove the glass, insert a new piece of glass that was the right size, and put the panels back together. The new panels were then shipped back to the construction site, and the thousands of defective glass panes were tossed into a dumpster and taken to the landfill.

Years later, when I started my academic career at Columbia University, I could admire my handiwork from my office window, more than ten miles away. The panels, it turned out, were for several floors of New York City's World Trade Center, and the lighted floors of the two 110-story towers were among New York's most recognizable landmarks. As I prepared to teach my classes, I always got a chuckle when I looked south toward the buildings, knowing that my summer work had produced a small—a very, very small—piece of those buildings.

Seven months after the buildings collapsed in the September 11, 2001, terrorist attacks, my wife and I visited "Ground Zero," the gaping, sixty-foot-deep wound in the ground that was all that remained of the towers. Plywood put up as a temporary part of the search and recovery process had become the place for memorials to the 343 firefighters and 60 police officers who died in the attacks. The street was filled with other people who had quietly come, as we had, to pay their respects to the more than 2,800 people who lost their lives there that September morning. Just the day before we visited, in fact, workers had discovered the remains of three more victims.

Three things struck us powerfully. The first was the enormous human toll. The poignant, personal notes from family members, posted on makeshift plywood walls around the historic St. Paul's Chapel, which had served as the headquarters and resting place for rescue workers, reminded everyone of the rich lives of those who died. The second was the sheer size of the disaster. Everyone had seen the site on television, but pictures of the sixteen-acre complex simply failed to capture its enormity. The third was the dust, which covered everything. In fact, the smell of wet dust—the removal teams had been spraying the debris with water for months to keep the dust from blowing around—was the first introduction to the site, even blocks away. It was impossible to escape the sense that the dust was the pulverized remains of the buildings and everything within them, including, in a small and ridiculously insignificant way, the fluorescent light panels on which I had worked as the towers were under construction.

The two big Boeing 767 jets that flew into the World Trade Center towers caused the biggest loss of life, but they were only part of the terrorist assault that morning. In an attack that was both exquisitely designed and horribly delivered, a third hijacked plane, American Airlines flight 77, flew into the Pentagon at such enormous speed that, according to engineering experts, the plane penetrated 310 feet of the building in less than a second.[1] The west side of the building collapsed, and the 64 people aboard the plane and 125 inside the Pentagon died. Among those who lost their lives were Leslie Whittington, a Georgetown University economist, her husband, and her two young daughters, who were on their way to Australia for a year-long sabbatical. Also killed was Lt. Gen. Timothy Maude, a thirty-four-year Army veteran who had developed the highly successful "Army of One" recruiting campaign.

On a fourth hijacked plane, which al Qaeda terrorist leaders later claimed was bound for the Capitol building in Washington, passengers learned through their cell phones that other planes had been hijacked and crashed in New York and Washington. Todd Beamer, a father of two from Cranbury, New Jersey, had called GTE Airfone operator Lisa Jefferson to tell her about the hijacking. "We're going to do something," Beamer told Jefferson, and he added simply, "I know I'm not going to get out of this." He asked the operator to pass along a message to his wife, Lisa: "Tell her I love her and the boys." Beamer asked Jefferson to recite the Lord's Prayer with him. When he had finished, Beamer asked a team of fellow passengers, "Are you guys ready?" He then said, "Let's roll." Listening intently, Jefferson heard screams, a struggle, and then she lost the connection.[2] Authorities later determined that Beamer and his colleagues rushed the cockpit and struggled with the hijackers to prevent another catastrophic attack. The plane fell from the sky into a field in Shanksville, Pennsylvania, hundreds of miles short of its intended target, killing all forty-four passengers and crewmembers aboard.

The next morning, editorial writers for the *New York Times* surveyed the crushing damage of the previous day's terrorist attacks. "It was, in fact, one of those moments in which history splits, and we define the world as 'before' and 'after,' " the editors sadly wrote. "We look back at sunrise yesterday through pillars of smoke and dust, down streets snowed under with the atomized debris of the skyline, and we understand that everything has changed." [3] Chris Patten, foreign affairs commissioner for the European Union, said, "This is one of the few days in life that one can actually say will change everything." [4] In the sad days after those horrendous attacks, from top officials to citizens on the street there seemed to be one common conclusion: Everything had changed. New York's *Daily News* observed, "Yesterday's explosions rocked the nation like an earthquake, with aftershocks that reached from coast to coast." [5]

Rarely do the nation's leaders face crises like the September 11 attacks. When observers concluded that the nation would never be the same again, they were also suggesting that the nation's leaders would have to rise to new levels—that they would have to frame new policies to prevent such attacks from ever occurring again. Everyone expected big changes in the realm of national security. As always happens in times of high national stress, the spotlight turned to the president, who bore the first responsibility for framing a response. Even more than that, citizens looked to the president for reassurance and strength.

When the planes slammed into the World Trade Center, President George W. Bush was in Florida to promote his education agenda. Chief of staff Andrew Card quietly came up to the president and whispered a quick bulletin about the attacks. Bush almost imperceptibly tightened his concentration, left the room, and headed for Air Force One, where his security aides knew he would be safe. Bush hopscotched around the country, ending up at an Air Force base in Kansas, where he assessed the situation. Against the wishes of some advisers, who worried about the possibility of more attacks, the president decided he needed to get back to Washington and speak to the nation. But his short speech that night—the first he would give from the Oval Office since becoming president—soon became known to his speechwriting staff as the "Awful Office" address. Speechwriter David Frum was dismayed, worried that the president had set precisely the wrong tone. Thinking about millions of Americans across the country, Frum later wrote, "I could imagine them thinking: Bush was a nice fellow, a perfectly adequate president for a time of peace and quiet; but this was war, real war, and he had given not one indication all day long of readiness for his terrible new responsibilities." [6]

The American people, rattled by the attacks and eager to strike out and strike back, were also eager for leadership. The attacks were the worst on American soil since Pearl Harbor. They were the first on the continental United States since the War of 1812. Americans looked to the president to explain what had happened and what would be done. But Bush was off his game and his staff knew it. The first day was not reassuring.

The president found sure footing just a few days later at an unscripted and impromptu event at Ground Zero itself. Just four days after terrorists flew planes into the World Trade Center towers, President Bush made a visit to the smoldering remains. With Air Force jets flying cover, he approached Ground Zero on Marine One, the presidential helicopter. Even though he had seen the devastation on television and had been thoroughly briefed on the disaster, he was amazed at the sickening smell of the still-burning buildings that crept into the cabin of his helicopter. He was even more shocked at the sheer size of the devastation.

That Saturday afternoon was gray. It had rained two days before, and drizzle had fallen on "the pile," as the towers' debris field had become known. The moisture mixed with dust and debris to create a slippery mess, which had already caused some rescuers to fall and suffer severe cuts. "It's like a big mudslide," said a Harvard medical student who was working at the site.[7] Bush clambered to the top of a pile of rubble, put his arms around a veteran New York firefighter, Bob Beckwith, and grabbed a bullhorn. "America today is on bended knee in prayer for the people whose lives were lost here, for the workers who work here, for the families that mourn." From the rowdy crowd of emergency workers came a shout, "I can't hear you." Bush used the megaphone to roar back, "I can hear you. The rest of the world hears you. And the people who knocked these buildings down will hear all of us soon."[8] The workers around him shouted their approval, pumped their fists in the air, and shouted, "USA! USA! USA!" Bush clambered down to shake hands with the rescue workers, toughened veterans who had seen unimaginable sights and who were visibly moved by the president's remarks.

From Ground Zero, Bush moved uptown to talk with two hundred relatives of missing police officers and firefighters. The president was scheduled for only a brief stop, but it turned into a touching, hour-and-a-half session. Family members pressed forward to ask Bush to sign photographs of their missing fathers, mothers, sons, and daughters. Arlene Howard gave the president the badge of her son, George Howard, a Port Authority police officer who died in the buildings' collapse.[9] During the first attack on the World Trade Center, in 1993, George Howard had helped rescue injured people. When the September 11 attacks occurred, it was his day off, but he rushed to the scene again. Howard lost his life trying to save people who were trapped.

The attacks focused national—and international—attention on Bush on precisely the issue—foreign policy and national defense—that his critics had long suggested he was least equipped to handle. It focused the attention of an anxious nation on him and his leadership as citizens asked, Is Bush up to the job? His trip to Ground Zero helped to silence that question. The unforgettable image of the president standing atop the pile of rubble with his arm around a firefighter and his meetings with the families of the fallen first responders gave Americans comfort at a time of deep loss and fear. Not only did Bush genuinely connect with the nation, but also, perhaps for the first time in his presidency, he found his voice.

Just four days after the World Trade Center fell, President Bush joined firefighter Bob Beckwith atop a burned fire truck to address a crowd of rescuers still searching for survivors. Bush's actions that day rallied public support and helped spark a sense of determination that built after the September 11 attacks.

Indeed, some of those close to him later suggested that in framing his response to the attacks he had discovered the fundamental purpose of his presidency.

"It's hard to describe what it's like to see the gnarled steel and broken glass and twisted buildings silhouetted against the smoke," Bush said that Saturday afternoon.[10] The way he wrestled with that sight—and the raw emotion it brought out—drew the best from Bush. It was a time of great stress for the nation and a wrenching test for Bush's leadership. Bush's impromptu speeches gave Americans what they wanted and needed from their president. Americans certainly had not forgotten the tense 2000 presidential election battle, its endless aftermath, and Bush's tiny victory. But perhaps for the first time, Americans—even partisan Democrats—were able to look past the electoral turmoil to accept Bush as their president. This was the day that the Bush presidency changed, fundamentally and forever.

Bush cemented his position when he spoke to a joint session of Congress a few days later. At the top of his game, Bush proudly told members of Congress and the national television audience that "the entire world has seen the state of our Union—and it is strong." He roused the audience by showing them George Howard's shield. "It is my reminder of lives that ended and a task that does not end," he declared. To thunderous applause, he said, "Tonight, we are a country awakened to danger and called to defend freedom. Our grief has turned to anger, and anger to resolution. Whether we bring our enemies to justice, or bring justice to our enemies, justice will be done." [11]

With the speech, Bush performed one of the president's most important jobs: he steadied a rattled nation. He refocused the administration's agenda, pushing other issues to the background so that he could concentrate on homeland security and the war against terrorism. He won support even from partisan Democrats on Capitol Hill, and his ratings in public opinion polls soared. Even his supporters admitted his first steps following the attacks had been wobbly. But fueled by his visit to Ground Zero, Bush found his voice and used it to set a crisp, new path for the nation—and for his presidency. "Bush's great gift to the country after September 11 was his calm and self-restraint," speechwriter David Frum explained later.[12] He shared the nation's grief, he calmed the nation's nerves, he framed a strategic response, and he projected a strong sense of leadership. Even critics grudgingly admitted that in the difficult weeks after September 11, he gave the nation just what it needed.

An event such as the September 11 attacks presents an unusual and important opportunity to examine how the American political system responds to big stresses. In many ways, the attacks worked in the same way as the stress tests that cardiologists give their patients. Doctors have long known that the best way to determine how well a person's heart works is to watch how well it performs under the stress of a treadmill at faster speeds and greater elevations. Under these conditions, a heart muscle that seems adequate in day-to-day activities can show signs

of weakness and breakdown. Political stresses likewise can reveal the inner work-
ings of the political system—what works well, what does not, and why.

In this book I will examine the results of the September 11 stress test for clues
about the underlying behavior and performance of American government. I will
examine the president's leadership, Congress's efforts to develop legislative solutions, the way the bureaucracy responded, and the critical links among the federal, state, and local governments. I will probe the underlying political values, especially civil rights and liberties, that shape the American political tradition. And
I will analyze the trade-offs implicit in the critical choices that shape American
policy. The nation's response to the attacks, as in all other important issues of
public policy, required setting a balance among important and competing objectives. After September 11, policymakers and citizens debated the proper balance
between presidential leadership and congressional debate, between national control and local discretion, between protection and liberty. The political stress test
thus is not only about how the system works—and how it sometimes does not. It
is even more fundamentally about the values that Americans must balance as they
make the critical decisions that determine the quality of national life.

THE RISE OF "HOMELAND SECURITY"

In the weeks that followed the attacks, Bush and his advisers devised a new strategy for "homeland security" and a new White House office to craft it. Bush ap-
pointed Pennsylvania governor Tom Ridge to head the new Office of Homeland
Security, and at Ridge's swearing-in ceremony Bush outlined his strategy. "We
will take strong precautions aimed at preventing terrorist attacks and prepare to
respond effectively if they might come again," he said. "We will defend our country; and while we do so, we will not sacrifice the freedoms that make our land
unique." [13]

The very phrase "homeland security" rankled some Americans. Critics suggested that the term sounded as if it had been derived from Hitler's Third Reich,
and others worried that it had an Orwellian, *1984* feel to it. In fact, according to
New York Times columnist William Safire, the word "homeland" had begun to
creep into the political lexicon during the early 1900s, as Zionists worked to establish a Jewish homeland in Palestine. Fascists in Austria and Germany later
picked up the term to refer to "homeland defense." In the United States, military
planners began thinking about "homeland defense" in 1997, but almost no one
noticed.[14] Conservatives began advancing the notion, and defense-oriented think
tanks explored what it would mean to prepare the nation for the possibility of
terrorism. It was not surprising, therefore, that when the Bush administration needed to respond quickly it used concepts—and a name—already in play.
There were other alternatives, such as the less ponderous "domestic security," but

policymakers reached for the term already in common (if narrow) use by experts and built their new policy around it.

At the core of the strategy was a series of dilemmas, which Bush's remarks captured. Bush pledged to prevent attacks, but he also pledged to be ready to respond if they occurred. He promised to defend the country without sacrificing liberty. The nation confronted the central, inescapable trade-off at the core of "homeland security": Achieving security against new, uncertain threats from terrorism inevitably meant giving up other things, including some freedoms. Just how much protection did the nation want? And how much sacrifice of civil rights and individual liberties would citizens tolerate in exchange for that protection?

That led administration officials to the central dilemma. They sought *prevention*: to do everything possible to ensure that those who might launch such attacks were stopped before they could try. But they also needed to strengthen *response*: to do everything possible, should an attack occur, to minimize injuries, the loss of life, and damage to property. Administration officials knew that any attack was unacceptable but that total protection was impossible. The terrorists had proved that they were cunning strategists who worked hard to identify and exploit points of vulnerability. Officials also were aware that they needed to strengthen the system's response. But that would matter only if the prevention strategy failed, and they did not want to talk publicly about that possibility. Officials thus needed to maximize their ability to respond while doing everything possible to prevent attacks in the first place.

For years, defense analysts had been warning that the nation needed a stronger strategy to prevent attacks. Just three months before the attacks, in fact, a coalition of defense think tanks staged an exercise at Andrews Air Force Base, just outside Washington, to explore the potential effects of a smallpox attack on the United States. Christened "Dark Winter," the exercise put experienced government officials—former senator Sam Nunn, D-Ga., for example, played the president—into a hypothetical situation and tracked their decisions.[15] The exercise suggested that as many as a million Americans might die from such an attack. Analysts concluded that the nation's leaders were ill-prepared for bioterrorism and that the health system did not have the capacity to deal with mass casualties.[16] As Nunn ominously told a congressional committee on July 23, 2001, after the "Dark Winter" exercise, "You often don't know what you don't know until you've been tested. And it's a lucky thing for the United States that—as the emergency broadcast network used to say: 'This is just a test, this is not a real emergency.' But Mr. Chairman, our lack of preparation is a real emergency."[17]

Indeed, earlier events had shown the need for a better national strategy to identify threats and prevent attacks, which were growing in number and destructiveness. The very same group of terrorists who launched the September 11 attacks had bombed the World Trade Center in 1993. Six people died in that attack and more than a thousand were injured. In Oklahoma City in 1995, an American, Timothy McVeigh, blew up the Murrah Federal Building and killed 168 people. In 2003 police arrested Eric Rudolph for the bombing of Atlanta's Centennial Park during the 1996 Summer Olympics. A May 2003 bombing of the Yale Law School, just days before graduation, hurt no one but made those attending the ceremonies very jittery.

Other nations have struggled for years with terrorists, from attacks in Israel during the Palestinian uprising to explosions staged by Northern Ireland partisans in London. A Japanese religious cult obsessed with a coming apocalypse released sarin, a nerve gas, in the Tokyo subway system in 1995. The attack miraculously killed only twelve, but it injured more than five thousand. In 1996 al Qaeda killed nineteen American servicemen in an attack on the Khobar Towers military barracks in Saudi Arabia. In 1998 the group simultaneously bombed the American embassies in Nairobi and Dar es Salaam. More than three hundred persons, including twelve Americans, died in those two attacks.

Disaffected groups have increasingly relied on terrorism, especially since the end of the cold war in the 1980s. Facing big and powerful military forces, the groups realized that small, focused, continuous attacks—especially attacks on civilians—could undermine governments and strengthen their position. An unrelenting terror campaign drove Russian troops out of Afghanistan, and groups in the Middle East began plotting more such attacks against American might. Handfuls of terrorists could not directly take on the American military, so they plotted what military analysts call "asymmetric attacks," bypassing the main military forces to inflict terror and pain, gain publicity, and deliver a message that no head-on military attack ever could.[18]

America's long-stated policy against negotiating with terrorists helped shape the terrorists' strategy. American officials determined never to be forced into bargaining with people who used violence to advance their goals. But if terrorists could not seize hostages and negotiate political deals, they found that they could use violence to promote their ideas and try to frighten nations that pursued policies they opposed. The resort to violence has also made terrorists more secretive, making it harder for government intelligence services to identify threats and uproot terrorist cells.

Meanwhile, new technologies have opened new avenues to terrorists. Weapons have become smaller and more portable. The miniature nuclear bomb that fits into a suitcase is an old device of spy novels. Although such a weapon is not feasible, it has become possible to put a nuclear bomb in a container small enough to be easily transported in a van. Microscopic bits of anthrax could kill hundreds, radioactive materials could injure thousands, and other biological and radiological weapons are also highly portable. After September 11, investigators discovered that Osama bin Laden and his al Qaeda terrorist cells communicated through highly sophisticated cellular phone networks and e-mail, even as bin Laden was hiding in primitive caves.

Small numbers of terrorists, armed with sophisticated weapons and even more sophisticated strategies, can stage bold attacks. America's massive military forces, which can defeat any army in the world, cannot guarantee protection against such tactics. Military forces, and the nation's homeland defense, can be very, very good. But 99.9 percent protection is not enough when terrorists can slip through tiny cracks in the system and inflict massive damage. It took just nineteen terrorists, armed with weapons that passed through metal detectors in at least four different airports, to stage the September 11 attacks.

Government officials obviously must do everything possible to prevent attacks, but they must also prudently plan to respond in case prevention fails. An effective response strategy consists of five missions:[19]

1. *Preparing government to assist civilians in case of attack.* On the morning of September 11, local firefighters and police officers had to answer the call first, and they faced the monumental task of evacuating tens of thousands of workers from the buildings attacked in New York and Washington. They had to provide first aid and medical attention, especially to severely burned casualties. They had to try to put basic infrastructure—water, electricity, telephone, and transportation—back together around Ground Zero. The first step in homeland security, therefore, is to help civilians who find themselves under attack. This is primarily a job for local governments.

2. *Providing for continuity of government.* As analysts studied the September 11 attacks, they realized that the nation's top leadership was vulnerable to such a carefully orchestrated series of strikes. Congress was in session that morning, and United flight 93, which crashed in Shanksville, seemed headed for the building. A catastrophic explosion could have killed or disabled many members of Congress and kept the legislature from working. Frantic Secret Service officers evacuated the White House complex, fearing that another plane was taking aim, and Vice President Cheney's security detail bodily picked him up and moved him to the White House's bomb shelter. Congress has long had a secret shelter attached to West Virginia's Greenbrier resort, but in the case of a terrorist attack there would be no warning to allow the members to get there. A blue-ribbon commission has warned about the need to ensure that the government can continue to function.[20] This is a job that all governments face.

3. *Providing for continuity of military operations.* Terrorist attacks also raise serious problems for control of the military's resources. Some terrorist attacks might demand an armed response. If civilian resources are overwhelmed, the military's troops and supplies might be needed. Defense planners have pointed out the need for military officials to ensure that their commanders and resources are not vulnerable to attack and do not themselves become targets. That is what happened on September 11 with the attack on the Pentagon. Defense officials focus on this job.

4. *Border and coastal defense.* The United States has a coastline stretching thousands of miles. The borders with Mexico and Canada stretch for thousands more. Long stretches of these borders lay across desolate territory and are mostly undefended. More than 5.7 million containers enter the nation's ports every year. Examining all of them is impossible, and analysts have long worried that explosives, biohazards, and even live terrorists could be smuggled into the country inside them. In 1999 a government customs official at the Washington-Canada border found an arms cache hidden inside a car and uncovered an attack planned for the eve of the millennium, possibly in Los Angeles. Analysts warned about the need for tighter control of the nation's borders and ports. They quickly realized that this was a job that required strong coordination among local governments, which operate ports; state governments that provide security; and the federal government, which operates the Coast Guard, the Bureau of Citizenship and Immigration Services (formerly the Immigration and Naturalization Service, or INS), and other border and coastal defense agencies.

5. *National air defense.* The final element of homeland security is also one of its oldest. The Air Force has long operated the North American Air Defense Command (NORAD) to detect missile or bomber attacks. During the cold war, NORAD focused its radars on the threat of an attack from the Soviet Union. Since September 11, it has taken on an expanded mission of protecting the domestic skies. The Defense Department has created a new "Northern Command," headed by a four-star general, to defend the skies over the United States and assist state and local governments if necessary. This is a new and expanded job for the military.

Ultimately, public officials pointed out, the nation's homeland defense depended on citizens as well. A government Web site, www.ready.gov, outlined the steps citizens should take. "Terrorism forces us to make a choice," it headlined. "Don't be afraid . . . be ready." What steps could citizens take? The Web site advised making a kit of emergency supplies, including a first aid kit and food and water; planning how to contact family members in an emergency; and becoming informed about what problems might occur. "With a little planning and common sense," the site advises, "you can be better prepared for the unexpected." Indeed, the focus on individual preparedness is what makes homeland security a truly unusual policy issue.

HOMELAND SECURITY AND PUBLIC POLICY

Citizens rely on government to manage the country's defense and foreign affairs, but the very nature of homeland security means that citizens can and must play a central role in their own safety. No matter how good a homeland security system the nation builds, it cannot be foolproof, and terrorists can find a way to exploit any vulnerability. Citizens anywhere may find themselves at risk, and they might have to rely on their own wits for safety. Homeland security poses huge new challenges for both government and citizens.

Citizens want strong leaders who can help them understand the threats they face and what they can do about them. In the days after September 11, the news media were full of stories posing the question, "Why do they hate us?" Reporters tried to fathom why the terrorists would willingly give their lives to kill and injure Americans they had never met, and why other foreigners would dig deep into their pockets to finance the operation. Understanding that the terrorists came from "failed societies that breed anger," as *Newsweek* put it, helped a bit.[21] But Americans were looking for more than just an intellectual explanation. They wanted—and needed—reassurance that the government was doing everything it could to prevent the September 11 attacks from recurring, as parents struggled to convince sleepless children that they were safe. The job of providing that reassurance fell to President Bush, and his speeches led to a soaring public approval rating of more than 90 percent, the highest ever recorded. (As memories of the September 11 attack became less fresh, however, his ratings fell back from these stratospheric levels.)

But Bush's personal popularity did not forestall questions by members of Congress, administration officials, journalists, and worried Americans about how the attacks happened and why they had not been prevented. Reformers sought big changes in national policy, especially because the investigations revealed the failure of federal intelligence officials to "connect the dots"—to put together the clues that something dangerous was afoot. The new homeland security debate extended to state and local governments, which found themselves financially stretched and administratively challenged to cope with new security demands. Local officials know that all homeland security problems are, first and foremost, local problems that demand a local response. They argued they could not protect their citizens without more financial help from the federal government.

The new homeland security strategy also raised tough questions about the trade-off between civil rights and security. It quickly became clear that stronger homeland security would require restrictions on individual civil rights and civil liberties. Efforts to prevent more hijackings, for example, led to far more careful screening of airline passengers and their baggage, and that produced far longer lines. Though by law passengers boarding airplanes have no expectation of privacy—a condition for protection under civil rights law—all travelers found themselves subject to much more intrusive screening. Many critics feared that security worries would lead to widespread intrusions into individual liberty, especially for travelers with Middle Eastern names or appearance. Federal officials have rounded up hundreds of individuals they suspect of having terrorist links and have held them for months without filing charges. Americans, who had long taken their rights and liberties for granted, found themselves confronting fundamental issues about how much freedom they were willing to sacrifice under the flag of security and how to ensure that security officials did not go too far.

Americans also had to learn how to think about risk differently. Experts reminded nervous fliers that even after September 11 they faced larger risks driving their cars to the airport than they did once in the air. But the attacks created a profound sense of vulnerability that shook many Americans to the core. For months, the *New York Times* devoted a page of the paper each day to "portraits of grief," short, touching vignettes of those who died at the World Trade Center.[22] They helped many Americans work through their grief, and they reminded readers that the attacks took the lives of thousands of ordinary Americans, of all races and incomes, who were going about their lives. The problem of vulnerability was especially intense for citizens of Washington and New York, where military jets flew combat patrols for months. In October 2001, the appearance of anthrax spores in letters had Americans across the country nervously checking their daily mail for suspicious white powder. Then, in February 2004, the discovery of the poison ricin in a U.S. Senate office building reminded Americans that the threat had not diminished. In fact, of course, most people were safe most of the time, but fear of another terrorist attack in the United States raised new questions about how safe people felt and how they viewed the role and performance of government.

Thus, on one level, America's new policy on homeland security is a story of how the nation—its government and its citizens—has dealt with the new specter of terrorism in the United States. Americans soberly sized up the reality that life would never again return to what it was on September 10, 2001. On a deeper level, the homeland security issue reveals how American government and society deal with stress. Just how does the system deal with a shock such as September 11? How much did the events of September 11 change the government? Did other events and other forces tug against those who wanted big changes and deep reforms? Doctors use a stress test to learn what works well and what does not, and they also use it to see how the heart bounces back after a heart attack. The stress test of September 11 likewise reveals not only the enduring realities that shape American government, but also the powerful forces that shape—and restrain— change. Is it true that "everything has changed"? More precisely, what has changed, what has not, and why?

Chapter

2

The System
Breaks Down

BUILT ALONG THE MAINE COAST, the setting of the Portland International Jetport is picturesque. Inside the modern terminal, airport security officials had long ago installed x-ray machines and a hidden surveillance camera system. On the morning of September 11, these cameras caught two young travelers carrying only light bags. The bags passed inspection and the two hurried to their plane for the short hop to Boston. Once in Boston, they had to rush to catch their connecting flight, American Airlines flight 11 to Los Angeles. Their connection was tight—they made it to their seats near the front of the plane, but their luggage was left behind on the tarmac. Inside these bags, detectives would later find a will and other papers suggesting the impending death of Mohammed Atta, who soon after takeoff led a team of five hijackers in taking over the two-aisle Boeing 767 aircraft.

Flight controllers overheard a mysterious message from the jet. "We have some planes," said a voice over the open radio. "Just stay quiet and you will be OK. We are returning to the airport." The transmission continued, "If you try to make any moves, you'll endanger yourself and the airplane." Inside the cockpit, the voice warned, "Just stay quiet." Flight attendant Betty Ong grabbed her cell phone and called American Airlines operations center. She told Craig Marquis, the manager on duty, that hijackers had seized the plane, that they had already killed one flight attendant, seriously wounded another, and slit a passenger's throat before storming the cockpit. Another flight attendant, Mary Amy Sweeney, reached Michael Woodward, an American Airlines manager back at Boston's Logan Airport, from which the plane had just taken off. Sweeney told him that the hijackers were armed with box cutters. The tool, sold in hardware stores, is a shirt-pocket-sized metal sheath holding a razor blade that slides out to open packing boxes. Controllers frantically tried to raise the crew on the radio but heard nothing. Anxious to figure out what was happening, Woodward asked flight attendant Sweeney where she was. Sweeney craned her head to look out the window and reported that she saw water and buildings. Radar tracks later showed that the plane had made a sudden turn to the south over Albany, New York, and picked up speed as it flew down the Hudson River toward Manhattan. Woodward heard Sweeney say, "Oh my God—oh my God," and then the plane, piloted by Mohammed Atta, crashed at almost top speed into the World Trade Center's North Tower.[1]

United flight 175, another Boeing 767, had also taken off from Boston just fourteen minutes after American flight 11. Soon after the plane left the ground, the pilot noticed something wrong. "We heard a suspicious transmission on our departure," the pilot radioed in. "Sounds like someone keyed the mike and said, 'Everyone stay in your seats.'"[2] Minutes later, the pilot found his cockpit overwhelmed by the same tactics that had hijacked American flight 11. Just as Atta had done, the hijackers cut off the radio and disconnected the transponder, which automatically broadcast the plane's location, direction, and speed. To the horror of Americans all over the country watching the North Tower inferno live on television, the hijacker at the controls, believed to be Atta's cousin Marwan Al-Shehri, took the plane on a looping turn and accelerated into the South Tower of the World Trade Center.

Two Boeing 757s, smaller planes than the ones that crashed into the World Trade Center towers, met similar fates. American flight 77 took off from Washington's Dulles Airport, bound for Los Angeles. Authorities suspect that the hijackers used box cutters to disable the crew, take control of the plane, and fly it into the Pentagon. A fourth team of hijackers seized United flight 93 and turned it toward the Capitol building in Washington. Air traffic congestion had delayed that plane's takeoff from Newark, which gave the passengers time to use their cell phones to learn the fate of the other planes. They were determined that their plane would not be used as a bomb and gave their lives in a frenzied rush to the cockpit. It was the only plane that did not reach the terrorists' intended target that morning.

In the days and weeks that followed, investigators struggled to determine what had happened—and how it had happened. There was a powerful sense that the nation's airport security system had broken down. Somehow, dangerous individuals had gotten dangerous weapons aboard the planes and had turned the planes themselves into weapons. Somehow, the intelligence services that were supposed to alert officials to threats had not detected the hijack plan. Somehow, the hijackers had discovered and exploited holes in America's security to disastrous effect. The system had failed, and cries arose across the country to fix it, to ensure that such a horrific attack could never recur.

The hijackers had passed through the security systems at four different airports. If the weapons in fact were box cutters and if the screeners had discovered them—there was no evidence that they did—they would have been powerless to confiscate them. Under Federal Aviation Administration (FAA) regulations, in place since a spate of hijackings using pistols in the early 1970s, passengers were

Early on the morning of September 11, two men, later identified by authorities as Mohammed Atta (right) and Abdulaziz Alomari (center), passed through security screening at Portland International Jetport. Minutes later, they took a commuter flight to Boston, where they boarded American Airlines flight 11. Soon after takeoff, they joined with three other hijackers to take over the plane and crash it into the World Trade Center's North Tower. This ghostly image of the two men coasting through security would later come to represent the apparent ease with which the hijackers exploited the gaps in airline security.

forbidden to carry "deadly" or "dangerous" weapons onto airplanes, but the box cutters did not meet that standard. Knives with blades less than four inches long, in fact, were legal, and the box cutters contained razor blades less than half that long. Many travelers carried pocketknives, and the FAA regulation seemed to recognize the practice. But the head of aviation policy for the General Accounting Office, Congress's investigative organization, said that the rule about knives "was always a puzzle to me." As Gerald Dillingham said a few days after the hijackings,

"I couldn't find an explanation of why 4 inches was acceptable. I'm still trying to find it."[3]

As investigators tracked the movements of the hijackers in the period before the attacks, they determined that several of them had taken previous test flights. They knew that they could sneak small blades onto aircraft. They carefully studied airline procedures, the routes and landmarks, and when the flight attendants began their meal service. They checked the security of the cockpits and found that the doors could easily be forced open. They found that morning flights were far more likely to be reliable than evening flights and that Tuesday flights, especially after the end of summer vacations, were often less crowded, which meant fewer passengers to be controlled. So, the hijackers decided to act on the morning of the second Tuesday in September in order to make it easier to synchronize their attacks. To maximize the explosions they were planning, they chose large planes fully fueled for transcontinental trips.

Within a few hours, federal investigators identified the September 11 hijackers and linked them to al Qaeda, an international terrorist ring responsible for the 1993 truck bombing of the World Trade Center. Having failed to cause sufficient damage in that first attack, al Qaeda's leader, Osama bin Laden, and his chief lieutenants determined to try again, this time with a more sophisticated plan targeted at the symbols of the New York financial center and the Washington political and military center. They hoped to inflict massive damage to the buildings. The collapse of both World Trade Center towers and the destruction of more buildings in the area were more than bin Laden had hoped for.

Fearing that yet more planes might be hijacked and turned into bombs, the Federal Aviation Administration (FAA)—for the first time in history—ordered all planes to land immediately at the nearest available airport. Passengers on transcontinental flights found themselves at small midwestern airports, and transatlantic flights crowded small Canadian airports. In St. John's, Newfoundland, where the airport typically saw just one small passenger plane land each day, twenty-seven jumbo jets full of 4,300 people landed. Tiny Gander, a Newfoundland town of ten thousand people, almost doubled its population within hours as thirty-nine jets landed. The Canadians proved generous hosts, even though the sudden influx strained their capacity to house and feed so many people. Grateful Americans later set up special scholarship funds for the children of those who had helped them.

The skies remained eerily empty for two days. For the first time in generations no aircraft—except military fighters on patrol—were in the air over the United States. Air operations gradually returned, but not to normal. Travelers faced tough new restrictions, from extra identification checks while boarding to extra screening of their luggage. Waits in security lines, which had lasted only minutes, now stretched into hours. Ronald Reagan National Airport, just across the Potomac River from Washington and within sight of the Capitol building, stayed closed for three weeks. When reopened, it operated with many fewer flights on highly restricted flight paths. Many Americans were afraid to fly, and airline traffic remained depressed for years following the attacks.

Everyone agreed that air travel security needed to be tighter. In fact, the long lines at airport checkpoints provoked few complaints, although airlines worried that the long lines would discourage already nervous fliers from returning to the air. Frequent fliers ridiculed some of the new regulations. They discovered that they could fly with nail clippers but not the tiny nail files attached to them. Security officials worried that the pointed files could become terrorist weapons. Members of Congress love Ronald Reagan National Airport, which they can reach from the Capitol in just ten minutes. Security officials had traced the flight paths of planes taking off and landing from Ronald Reagan National's main runway, however, and had determined that the White House and Capitol were just seconds away—and that they would have virtually no chance of stopping a plane that suddenly veered off course. Consequently, the airport closed down, and members of Congress had to travel more than an hour to one of the area's two other airports.

If the extra security proved reassuring, it also proved inconvenient, expensive, and crippling to some businesses. Powerful pressures began building across the country to ensure that the emphasis on security did not choke business and freedom. Everything had changed—but it also became clear that some of the changes would not be permanent. No one wanted to chance another hijacking, but questions quietly began surfacing: Had the government gone too far, from banning tiny nail files to closing Ronald Reagan National Airport? New rules aimed at strengthening security, but old forces pushed back. Where and how would government set the balance?

The attacks presented a stunning challenge to the American system. A well-functioning bureaucracy coordinates complex activities into seamless services. If the system's designers fail to anticipate possible loopholes, or if the system's operations fail to close them, serious problems can develop. For the vast array of relatively routine government programs, from mailing Social Security checks to putting out fires, long years' experience usually makes the system smooth and well functioning. But the September 11 attacks presented the system with new tests and found cracks that officials had not anticipated. These cracks widened and spread from the failure to detect and prevent the attacks to the efforts of state and local officials to respond to them. They caused difficulty in dealing with an unexpected second terror wave of anthrax attacks and with yet another new threat from a terrorist with a bomb hidden in his shoes. In this chapter, we will examine the imposing difficulty of designing and managing an effective homeland security system and the consequences that can flow from failure. Like any good stress test, these issues help chart the system's manifest strengths as well as its points of vulnerability.

CONNECTING THE DOTS

The spotlight quickly focused on the nation's intelligence services. Who were these hijackers, and how could the intelligence agencies have failed to detect their plot? In fact, investigators learned that many clues had emerged in the months before the attacks. Other clues lay undiscovered. Even worse, the intelligence agencies had failed to piece together the clues they did have. The refrain came to be repeated over and over: Why had the intelligence agencies failed to connect the dots?

Investigators first focused on determining who the hijackers were, as that would give them a clue to where the attacks had come from. Aboard one of the planes, a flight attendant had managed to identify the seat numbers where some of the hijackers had been sitting. A check against the boarding manifest gave investigators the hijackers' names to add to the fragmentary intelligence they had collected before the attacks and the telephone communications intercepted later that day. In relatively short order, they identified the likely hijackers, and just as quickly they determined that the men were members of al Qaeda.

In Mohammed Atta's luggage, investigators found his will. In several cars rented by the hijackers, handwritten lists of rules, including "Be calm" and "You are carrying out an action God loves" were found. Atta and other hijackers had wired thousands of dollars back to the United Arab Emirates in the days before the attacks, and Atta had visited an ATM machine, a gas station, and a Wal-Mart the night before. Atta and a fellow hijacker on the American Airlines flight had slept at a Portland Comfort Inn. The cleaning staff reported later that the hijackers had slept on top of the sheets—and left behind a bathroom floor full of body hair. Investigators believed that was part of their preparation: a smooth body would enable them to pass more easily into the afterlife.[4]

In a disquieting near miss just two days before the attacks, a Maryland state policeman pulled over Ziad Jarrah on Interstate 95 near the Delaware border. Jarrah was doing 90 in a 65 mile-per-hour zone, and State Police colonel David B. Mitchell issued him a $270 ticket. Investigators found the ticket in the car's glove compartment at the Newark airport and a fragment of Jarrah's passport in the Shanksville wreckage. They believe that Jarrah was the pilot of the fourth plane, bound for the Capitol.[5]

Even more startling, investigators discovered that several of the hijackers had received flight training in the months before the attacks. According to their instructors, none was an especially good pilot. Atta had once simply walked away from a plane at a Miami airport instead of parking it properly. Hani Hanjour, one of the hijackers who crashed the American Airlines jet into the Pentagon, claimed to have had six hundred hours of flight experience, but his Maryland flight instructors found he flew so poorly that they would not let him solo.[6] A Scottsdale,

Arizona, flight instructor said that Hanjour had missed flights and skipped homework assignments. Another Pentagon hijacker trained in San Diego.

As investigators uncovered the trails of the hijackers, they began to build evidence about who they were, how they were trained, and where they had gotten their money. They discovered a common link to earlier al Qaeda operations, including Ramzi Yousef's role in the 1993 World Trade Center bombing and in a complex plan to blow up twelve American jetliners simultaneously over the Pacific. Yousef, intelligence officials knew, had also received flight training in the United States, and they knew that he had considered flying a hijacked plane into the headquarters of the Central Intelligence Agency (CIA). Intelligence had uncovered previous al Qaeda operations, as well as plans to turn planes into bombs. They knew that some terrorists had sought flight training, and they suspected that more attacks might be in the works. But they failed to collect enough information about the September 11 operation in time to act.

Some Federal Bureau of Investigations (FBI) field agents, in fact, had worried that al Qaeda operatives were getting flying lessons and might be preparing new attacks. Two months before the September 11 hijackings, Phoenix FBI agent Kenneth Williams warned his superiors that Middle Eastern students at a nearby flight school might be members of al Qaeda preparing for hijackings. Agents in Minneapolis warned their superiors that Zacarias Moussaoui, a French citizen, was taking flight lessons.[7] Congressional investigators were stunned to learn that the FBI had identified two suspicious flight training programs but had not acted. There was no evidence that top FBI officials learned of all these warnings until after the September 11 attacks. Lower-level officials were sorting out competing leads, and the Phoenix and Minneapolis warnings did not receive serious attention until after the attacks. That worried Sen. Charles Grassley, R-Iowa, who pointedly asked, "What will it take to 'connect the dots' necessary to piece together obscure clues and pursue leads to prevent another September 11 from devastating America all over again?"[8] Led by Grassley and Sen. Bob Graham, D-Fla., members of Congress asked out loud why intelligence officials failed to connect the dots—why federal officials had not assembled the clues in a way that would have helped them detect and prevent the attacks.

The deeper they dug, the more evidence congressional investigators found that terrorists were considering the use of airplanes for staging terrorist attacks. As early as 1994, intelligence experts had learned that terrorists planned to crash an Air France jet into the Eiffel Tower. Four years later, in August 1998, intelligence officials uncovered evidence that Arab terrorists were planning to fly an explosives-laden plane into the World Trade Center and that Osama bin Laden was actively considering terrorist strikes in the United States, possibly in New York and Washington. But the intelligence agencies did not produce any analysis on how much of a threat bin Laden might be or the risk that the nation faced from the use of airplanes as flying bombs. A 2002 congressional investigation concluded that "there was apparently little, if any, effort by Intelligence Community analysts to produce any strategic assessments of terrorists using aircraft as weapons." But intelligence officers also had mountains of other suspicious activities to assess, including threats to public buildings that were proven groundless. So despite some information pointing to the contrary, after sorting through all the intelligence less than a year before the September 11 attacks, the FBI had estimated that the risk of attack through civil aviation was low.[9]

Congressional investigators found that, despite mounting evidence collected by the intelligence agencies, the agencies failed to share the information they had with each other. No agency had the whole picture, but the pieces collected before September 11 painted an interesting, albeit inconclusive, picture. The FBI did not share what it had with the CIA, and neither adequately shared information with the State Department, whose consular offices could have prevented the terrorists from entering the country if they had been warned. The National Security Agency had other information, but the agency was not linked adequately to the FBI, CIA, and State Department. "It is a colossal intelligence failure," Mary Ryan, head of the State Department's Bureau of Consular Affairs, said a month after the attacks. For example, the State Department issued Atta a visa to enter the country in May 2000, even though other intelligence officials had collected evidence that he had met with key al Qaeda officials five months earlier.[10] In their 2002 report, congressional investigators pointedly asked why the agencies had not shared information with each other.

The investigators found that immigration officials had lost track of the hijackers after they entered the country and that the terrorist teams had assembled an impressive array of identification cards. On the morning of September 11, three of the hijackers had expired visas and thus were in the country illegally, but airline ticket agents had no way of knowing this. Some investigators believed that the nineteen hijackers held a total of sixty-three driver's licenses.[11]

The congressional investigation also found that the super-secret National Security Agency, which intercepts electronic communications, had in 1999 listened in on conversations between two future hijackers and discovered that they were linked to a suspected al Qaeda facility. The National Security Agency (NSA) did not share this information with other intelligence agencies. Meanwhile, the CIA independently learned of the men's al Qaeda connections, but it did not share the information with immigration officials who could have prevented them from entering the country. The FBI had developed an informant who lived with two of the future hijackers, but its officials did not learn of what the CIA knew until after September 11. Had the agencies linked what they knew, it is possible that these hijackers could have been kept out of the United States, that the FBI could have used its informant to learn more about the developing plot, or at least that the intelligence agencies could have investigated further.

The post–September 11 investigations revealed that although government agencies kept a dozen different "watch lists" of suspicious individuals, officials had not coordinated the information they contained. The General Accounting Office found that the watch lists "include overlapping but not identical sets of data, and different policies and procedures govern whether and how these data are shared with others."[12] The government had collected vast quantities of data on possible threats, but the agencies simply had not cooperated to piece together a coherent picture from the fragments collected.

In short, as Senators Grassley and Graham pointed out, the problem lay in *connecting the dots*. Investigators did not find any smoking guns—clear, incontrovertible evidence—that showed senior officials knew enough about the plans for the September 11 attacks in advance to be able to prevent them. But the investigators did find a large number of tantalizing clues that, if connected, would have provided evidence for the need to take decisive action. In surveying the information they collected, investigators also determined that the United States remained highly vulnerable to further attacks. Osama bin Laden, among others, vowed more strikes.

The conclusion was that unless the government did a far better job of coordinating efforts, the nation risked further catastrophes. With better preparedness, officials might be able to prevent the attacks or, at the very least, greatly reduce the damage if they occurred. Senator Graham summed up the findings, "If there had been more cooperation and sharing of information, if there had been more creativity, and some luck, this plot could have been discovered well before it resulted in September the 11th."[13] The system broke down not so much because the government had not collected the information but because its agencies failed to share and digest the information they had. Congressional investigators found that both sad and infuriating. They made connecting the dots—the need to coordinate intelligence—into a national watchword.

MYSTERIOUS POWDER

Americans had barely caught their breath when, three weeks after the September 11 hijackings, a sixty-three-year-old Florida photo editor died from inhaling anthrax. The substance is a natural bacterium that often occurs on farms and rarely is harmful to people in this natural state, although it has caused widespread deaths among livestock. Government weapons experts have long known that the spores can be grown in a laboratory, purified and concentrated, and separated into tiny microscopic dust just one twenty-fifth the thickness of a piece of toilet paper. The dust can then be made into an aerosol that hangs in the air and can be easily inhaled. In its early stages, anthrax affects the lungs like a common cold, and antibiotics can treat it effectively. But once the toxin spreads, the lungs fill with suffocating fluid. The body goes into shock, and the disease is 90 percent fatal.

Investigators at first suspected that the photo editor, Robert Stevens, might have contracted anthrax from a natural source. Florida officials said that there was no cause for alarm and that it was probably just an isolated case. They said they were carefully examining the circumstances but were not treating it as a criminal case. All of that changed dramatically when investigators discovered that a letter passing through his company's mailroom contained anthrax and that his work area was contaminated. They found more anthrax in a nearby postal facility. A second worker in Stevens's building, Ernesto Blanco, came down with anthrax. Doctors caught Blanco's infection early and treated him with heavy doses of Cipro, an antibiotic highly effective against anthrax. Blanco survived.

Soon, cases of anthrax began popping up across the East Coast. An assistant to Tom Brokaw, anchor for the *NBC Nightly News,* contracted the skin-based version of anthrax. The substance had entered the newsroom in an envelope, and three other people who handled the envelope contracted anthrax as well. At ABC, the seven-month-old son of a news producer came down with the skin-based form. So did an assistant to CBS anchor Dan Rather and an employee at the *New York Post.* Anthrax turned up in the New York City office of Gov. George Pataki and in four sorting machines in Manhattan's largest mail distribution center. A hospital worker went to the hospital on October 29 with what authorities suspected was inhalation anthrax. She died two days later.

The cases spread to Washington, D.C., where twenty staffers in the office of Senate Majority Leader Tom Daschle, D-S.D., tested positive for anthrax. At the Brentwood mail processing facility, which processes most of the mail for the Washington area—including the Capitol—two postal workers died. The contamination forced the closure of the facility until late 2003 and the rerouting of hundreds of thousands of pieces of mail. More anthrax turned up at the State Department, the Supreme Court's off-site mailroom, the Department of Health and Human Services (HHS), and in a letter addressed to Sen. Patrick Leahy, D-Vt. Additional cases appeared in New Jersey, and a few weeks later, a ninety-four-year-old Connecticut widow, whose mail apparently went through the sorting machines at about the same time as other anthrax-laced mail, died.

In all, the anthrax attacks killed five people and sickened seventeen. With major New York news organizations and Washington politicians as targets, the attacks seemed to have been planned to maximize publicity. The Postal Service posted tips about how to handle suspicious mail.[14] The September 11 bombings were against prominent targets, but the seeming randomness of the anthrax infections—a photo editor working at his desk, a widow reading her mail, a baby visiting an office—terrified already shaken Americans. Officials warned schools to establish policies in case a worrisome package arrived, and many businesses put similar policies into place.

Emergency officials across the country found themselves swamped with calls about suspicious powders. A small bit of vanilla pudding caused the evacuation of a building in Albuquerque. Monterey, California, police discovered that a suspicious substance outside a hotel was spilled mango juice. Another was bird droppings on a driveway. A worried New Jersey resident called 911 because a piece of Halloween candy burned his tongue. A state police trooper carefully collected the suspicious candy and sent it to the state police laboratory for careful analysis, where lab workers found that it was, in fact, just Halloween candy. New Jersey state police officers responded to more than 3,500 false alarms in the first month after the attacks started. Most came from citizens who worried they could be next. Some were deliberate hoaxes. More than two hundred family planning and abortion clinics received envelopes signed from the "Army of God," containing suspicious white powder and markings that said, "This is anthrax. Now you die." [15]

Officials and intelligence analysts feared a second wave of attacks, but they did not know what form such attacks might take. When anthrax arrived on the scene, they did not know whether it came from al Qaeda or some other source. Officials discovered that Mohammed Atta had taken flight training a short distance from the photo editor's office and that the terrorists had explored the use of crop dusters to spread harmful chemical or biological agents. It was hard to believe that the timing of the anthrax attacks was coincidental. Moreover, the focus on Washington officials and New York media stars matched al Qaeda's operating style. Analysts determined that the anthrax was of high quality, which suggested that whoever spread the spores was highly skilled and had access to sophisticated equipment. Yet after years of exhaustive laboratory and field work, which included draining a pond near a suspect's home, they were unable to determine who had spread the anthrax. They could not determine whether the anthrax came from foreign or domestic sources, whether it had been supplied by a hostile nation such as Iraq or had come from a disgruntled worker at a federal installation. They believed that only a relative handful of people—or governments—were capable of producing the kind of spores they found. But they could not determine who had mailed the powder.

Despite the failure to identify the source of the anthrax, officials knew that the attacks underlined the bigger message—everything had changed. Analysts worried that the threats had changed but the government's capacity had not. In particular, they were concerned that the attacks revealed new and serious problems of coordination. Across the country, fire and police officials found themselves swamped with false alarms. When a few cases proved genuine, the system was slow to respond, and some infected victims did not get Cipro treatment in time. Without better coordination, future attacks might bring more devastating casualties.

Before September 11, intelligence analysts well understood the possibility and risks of biological and chemical attacks. The Japanese terrorist group Aum Shinrikyo had already conducted a sarin attack and another in which it sprayed anthrax from a rooftop and a van. American experts had conducted exercises on the impact such attacks might have in the United States. In October 1999, ABC's

Nightline aired a five-part series on the implications of an attack on the Washington subway. Its "Biowar" investigation began with the hypothetical smashing of a jar of anthrax on the subway's tracks. Within eight days, according to the show's consultants, the death toll might well have reached fifty thousand, and the region's health care system would have been overwhelmed.[16] Local officials had studied the problem as well. In August 2001, officials in Madison, Wisconsin, planned an exercise to test the local response to an anthrax attack. The exercise, scheduled for October, was canceled when officials were overwhelmed by hundreds of calls from worried residents who were finding suspicious powder.

Given the potential of anthrax to kill thousands, officials quietly breathed a sign of relief that the October attacks were limited to five deaths. They found that an effective anthrax attack proved hard to stage and, if treated quickly with antibiotics, easy to stop. But they also found that the biological attack, coupled with the extra security put in place after September 11, badly strained state and local governments. As Mayor John DiStefano of New Haven, Connecticut, explained a year later, "In an environment where 40-odd states are experiencing budget deficits and oftentimes solving those deficits, in part, on the backs of cities and towns, you're getting communities that are stressed by the increased demand to provide security services." The strain was wearing on cities, said Washington, D.C.'s emergency management director, Steve Charvat. "They're lucky if they can do the bread-and-butter type disaster plans, much less everything that's been thrown on their plate since 9/11."[17]

State and local agencies discovered their own connect-the-dots problems. The terrorist attacks posed new challenges for state and local officials, who had to put their police and fire departments on overtime. They also had to devise new strategies for coping with hypothetical problems, since these may one day be reality. And they quickly realized that they needed to do far more to coordinate local emergency workers into integrated teams. No longer was terrorism the concern of just a handful of big cities. Officials around the country had to face the possibility that the mail could bring terrorism to their doorsteps and that, in any event, worried citizens might swamp their emergency services with false alarms. They discovered that they needed to connect their own dots and to find new ways of paying for vastly more difficult and complex services.

WORRIES SPREAD

Nervous travelers became even edgier on December 22, 2001, only days before Christmas. On American Airlines flight 63 from Paris to Miami, passengers were just finishing lunch when a terrified woman's shriek broke the calm. A passenger in a window seat, Richard Reid, was lighting matches and holding them to a fuse protruding from his sneaker. Two flight attendants struggled with Reid, and other passengers jumped up to stop him, some contributing their belts to restrain him.

The crew sedated Reid with drugs from the first aid kit, and a basketball player towered over him for the rest of the flight to ensure that he did not move from his seat. No one was sure that Reid did not have accomplices on board—after all, the September 11 hijackers had traveled in groups. Accompanied by military jets, the plane diverted to Boston, where it landed safely and passengers quickly evacuated the plane.[18]

The FBI took Reid into custody and examined his sneakers. They discovered that the shoes were packed with enough explosives to blast a large hole in the plane's fuselage and probably blow it out of the sky. Investigators found no accomplices, but they did find links between Reid and al Qaeda. They found that Reid had received training in bin Laden's Afghan camps and that al Qaeda had developed shoe bombs in the past. The bomb was sophisticated, and the FBI found hair and palm prints on the shoe that did not belong to Reid. They concluded that he had to have had help, and thus it was likely that he was part of a larger terrorist network. They also worried that Reid had not appeared in earlier terrorist investigations and that, if he had succeeded, the 767 jetliner might simply have dropped into the ocean, leaving behind few clues. Even though the United States had attacked Afghanistan in October 2001 and quickly toppled the Taliban regime there, top officials realized that al Qaeda had trained many terrorists who had scattered around the world. Destroying the central headquarters would not destroy the rest of the network.

At that point, in late 2001, aviation security officials had dramatically increased the screening of passengers and their carry-on luggage and had strengthened the background checks of airline employees and before-flight computer checks of passengers. With the new worry that terrorists might use suicide shoe bombs, passengers were asked to remove their shoes and put them through security screening. Passengers complained about the continued inconvenience. As a Seattle Internet consultant grumbled, "The other night, they had everybody taking off their shoes—grandmothers surrendering their wooden clogs and teenagers taking off their Chuck Taylors."[19]

In early 2002, Americans learned they also needed to worry about "dirty bombs." Attorney General John Ashcroft announced the arrest of Abdullah Al Mujahir, an American citizen and a member of a Chicago street gang, as he entered the United States. Ashcroft said that Al Mujahir was suspected of being involved in a plan to detonate a "dirty bomb," a conventional explosive mixed with radioactive materials. It was not a nuclear weapon, but if exploded it could spread radioactivity over a neighborhood. Such a bomb, experts estimated, could kill thousands, sicken thousands more, and contaminate the neighborhood for a long time. Indeed, American officials suspected the contamination and fear factor might well prove to be such a bomb's biggest impacts. As *Time* magazine correspondent Mark Thompson explained, "any bomb that killed people and set off Geiger counters would terrify a whole city. It's ultimately a pure terror weapon."[20]

American officials believed that any plot was in its earliest stages. They transferred Al Mujahir to a naval base and held him in custody as an "enemy combatant."

American intelligence officials knew that al Qaeda and other terrorists had been working for some time to obtain radioactive materials. Obtaining such material would be much easier than buying actual nuclear weapons, although officials worried that the collapse of the Soviet Union might have made a few nuclear bombs available to terrorists. A dirty bomb did not require much sophisticated equipment. A wide variety of nuclear materials, from old power plants or medical uses, could be coupled with a truck bomb, such as the ones that al Qaeda used against the World Trade Center in 1993 and that Terry Nichols used in 1995 in Oklahoma City, to kill large numbers of people and spread radioactivity. Officials later concluded that the dirty bomb plot had not advanced past the discussion stage and that no attack was imminent. But Al Mujahir's arrest added one more dimension to the mosaic of homeland defense problems confronting American governments at all levels.

In fact, the very complexity of the problem and of the range of possible threats itself proved daunting. New problems emerged at a dizzying rate. The public did not know which things to worry about most or, indeed, how much to worry. Officials were concerned about dangerous gaps both in preventing and responding to attacks. Because the terrorists were relying on "asymmetric" attacks, in which small numbers of terrorists could inflict great devastation, the problem loomed even larger. Attacks could come anywhere, at any time, through any of a wide variety of routes. They targeted civilians as well as symbols in ways guaranteed to attract the broadest possible public attention and to put citizens and their governments off guard. Intelligence officials learned that al Qaeda operatives believed that the United States was contaminating Islamic culture and supporting governments (such as Saudi Arabia's) that were subverting the core of the Islamic religion. By inflicting damage on American territory, the terrorists hoped to drive the United States out of the Middle East and to undermine the American way of life. It was as large a shock as the United States had suffered since the Japanese attack on Pearl Harbor in 1941. It also foreshadowed a change in the policies and processes of American government—and American life—that would be even bigger.

New threats had emerged, and citizens were understandably more anxious. They had to find new ways of coping with threats that were both unpredictable and frightening. The government's intelligence operations had to devise new methods to prevent attacks. State and local agencies discovered serious problems in responding to attacks once they occurred—or to citizens' fears about false alarms. State and local officials complained that federal officials were not providing enough information. Federal officials worried that state and local officials were not sufficiently coordinated to provide an effective response. They were concerned that police officers were not working closely enough with firefighters, that firefighters were not closely linked to emergency medical technicians, that public health workers expert in biological threats were not called in soon enough—that, in short, there were too many gaps in the system through which too many people might be hurt or killed.

HOMELAND SECURITY AS COORDINATION

Homeland security, at its core, is about coordination. It is not only about developing new tools but—more fundamentally—weaving together far more effectively the nation's existing experts and resources. It is a matter of doing some new things, many old things much better, and some old things differently, all in an environment that can punish any mistakes severely.

At the same time, none of the nation's other goals and aspirations has gone away. Citizens still expect good local schools, quality colleges and universities, regular delivery of Social Security checks, and high environmental quality. They expect good roads, effective snow removal, and trash pick up. They want safe streets, quick emergency care in case of an accident, and a fire department that will promptly extinguish flames. They want national parks to preserve beauty and a safe food supply. With the rise of homeland security as a concern, none of the old policy imperatives has evaporated. New ones have only been added.

The country can spend almost limitless amounts of money and impose extraordinary costs and still not prevent a clever terrorist from finding a crack in the system. At the same time, a streamlined, well-designed system can frustrate most terrorist schemes. The key to an effective homeland security system is, in fact, connecting the dots—ensuring strong coordination among those responsible for prevention and those charged with response. No single agency, no single level of government—indeed, no government itself, without the active partnership of its citizens—can hope to forestall attack. Should an attack occur, no one agency, level of government—or even government itself—can adequately respond. Homeland security is, indeed, at its core a problem of coordination.

As Harold Seidman pointed out, coordination is the "philosopher's stone" of government's work. Medieval alchemists believed that if they could find this magic stone, they would find the answers to human problems. Coordination, Seidman argues, has the same appeal for public officials today. "If only we can find the right formula for coordination," he wrote, "we can reconcile the irreconcilable, harmonize competing and wholly divergent interests, overcome irrationalities in our government structures, and make hard policy choices to which no one will disagree."[21]

"Coordination" is a diagnosis of the homeland security problem. Terrorists work by trying to identify and exploit gaps in the system. It is also a diagnosis of the solution: improved homeland security is a matter of strengthening coordination, in both preventing and responding to attacks. In each case, identify the dots that must be connected and the problems will be solved.

This applies not just to detecting and preventing terrorist attacks. It applies as well to ensuring an effective local response to terrorist events. When such events occur, they place big demands on local first responders—police officers, firefighters, emergency medical technicians, public health workers, and others—who arrive on the scene. Big terrorist events, like the attacks on the World Trade Center and the Pentagon, require extraordinary levels of coordination. Even smaller events, however, like the tragic crash of United Flight 93 into a Pennsylvania field, required response from several neighboring communities. Such events are not simply fires, crime scenes, or places with injured people. They can happen all at once and can swamp the ability of any agency or any jurisdiction to respond. Hence, the effectiveness of a community's response to a terrorist event depends on the level of coordination it can marshal. And since terrorist events, almost by definition, are sudden shocks, such coordination depends on putting response plans into place long before the event.

That was just the case in Arlington County, Virginia, where local first responders confronted the crash of American Airlines flight 77 into the Pentagon. At 9:37 A.M., Captain Steve McCoy and his crew aboard Engine 101 were traveling to a training session on Interstate 395 near the Pentagon. They were talking about the tragedy at the World Trade Center. Suddenly they saw a jetliner in a steep dive bank sharply before disappearing in a thunderous explosion. From their location, McCoy and his crew could not determine where the plane had crashed, but another team of firefighters already on duty at the Pentagon barely escaped the explosion and radioed the location. The plane had been traveling at 400 miles per hour, close to its maximum speed, and had penetrated the first three of the building's five rings. Soon McCoy and his crew, along with hundreds of other first responders from the area, were at the scene.

Within minutes, well-practiced emergency plans went into effect. Fire and rescue units from nearby Ronald Reagan Washington National Airport sped to the scene, as did other units from across Arlington County. The FBI's Washington Field Office dispatched its response team. The first units arrived on the scene within two minutes of the attack. Fire department commanders established their headquarters within four minutes, and the FBI arrived within five minutes. The area's hospitals were ready to receive the injured within twelve minutes.[22] The fire chief of neighboring Alexandria sent a battalion chief to the Arlington command post to say, simply, "Anything you need, you've got."[23] For the next ten days, the county's emergency operations staff remained on the scene to conduct search and rescue operations.

A few months later, the county asked a private consultant to evaluate its performance. The consultant's report found the response exemplary—"ordinary men and women performing in extraordinary fashion."[24] Coordination efforts proved to be "a model that every metropolitan area should emulate." The county responded so well—and its coordination with the FBI and neighboring governments worked so effectively—because of the leadership the county's emergency services officials had shown in the years leading up to the attacks. "Leadership isn't learned in a day," the consultants argued, "it is learned every day." [25] Among other things, Arlington County officials had carefully framed an emergency response plan built on an integrated command structure, mutual aid agreements with surrounding communities, a solid emergency team, an assistance program to back up employees amid the stress of their work, and constant drilling over several years. The response, the consultants said, "was successful by any measure." Loss of life was minimized, and "Had it not been for the heroic actions of the response force and the military and civilian occupants of the Pentagon, clearly the number of victims would have been much higher." [26]

The coordination extended to the region's health authorities. Many of the most badly injured victims had suffered severe burns, and the area's hospitals soon ran short of skin grafts. The usual procedure would be to fly in the replacement skin from another location, but because of the attacks all flights in the nation were grounded. Medical officials created a nonstop relay of drivers to transport seventy square feet of skin from Texas to Washington. Local police officers in jurisdictions along the way provided escorts to speed the emergency supplies along, itself an extraordinary feat of coordination. [27]

By contrast, the attacks on the World Trade Center produced staggering coordination problems. [28] Commanders in the lobbies of the two towers lacked reliable information about what was happening above them or outside the buildings. In fact, horrified television viewers around the country had better information on the spread of the fires than the lobby commanders, who had no access to the television broadcasts. Radio communications were sporadic throughout the towers. A New York City Police Department helicopter circled overhead, but the fire chiefs had no link to the police information. There were no senior NYPD personnel at the fire department's command posts—and vice versa. Desperate to help their comrades, some firefighters raced up the stairs without waiting for orders, but that made it impossible for New York City Fire Department (FDNY) officers to track who was at the scene.

The FDNY had no established process for securing mutual aid from surrounding communities. Both Nassau and Westchester counties supplied ad hoc assistance, but the FDNY had no procedure for integrating the reinforcements into its own effort. With half of the FDNY force at the World Trade Center, and with no established mutual aid agreement with neighboring communities, the rest of the city was left with perilously thin protection. Almost all of the city's special operations units, such as hazardous materials and rescue teams, were at the World Trade Center, leaving few resources to respond had another major event occurred.

New York City's consultant found that although the FDNY had previously considered many strategies to enhance coordination, it had "never fully brought them to fruition." The consultant pointedly concluded, "Success will be predicated on managers, civilian and uniformed, who are committed to bringing about profound change, are capable of leading all personnel by example and are eager to embrace full accountability for their own performance."[29] The consultant warned that even after the attacks there were few signs that the department's leaders had taken the steps necessary to secure better coordination, especially with the police department.

First responders raced into burning buildings without regard to their own safety, but the scale of the New York attacks swamped the system. After the attacks, however, investigators found that deep-seated rivalries, especially between the NYPD and the FDNY, had prevented the two departments from sharing critical information on the morning of the attack. Coordination problems within the departments, especially the FDNY, might have increased the death toll among firefighters. The local response systems proved just as susceptible to bureaucratic competition and coordination problems as the intelligence community was in dealing with the disconnected early clues it received about the hijackers' activities.

It must be said, in fairness, that the two local situations were very different. The New York attacks involved two buildings, not one. The buildings' collapse and the resulting fires involved sixteen blocks, destroyed all seven buildings in the World Trade Center complex, and seriously damaged many more. A forty-story skyscraper across the street from the South Tower, owned by Deutsche Bank, was so badly damaged that officials decided to demolish it. The fires were fueled by the tanks of planes far larger than the one that crashed into the Pentagon, and the tall, thin World Trade Center towers created a far more difficult evacuation problem than the broad, low Pentagon building. Any emergency system would have struggled with the sheer scale of the New York attacks, and in the view of many experts, New York's emergency system is perhaps the best in the world.

Public officials, especially in Washington, concluded that they had to do something to prevent further attacks and, should any occur, to improve the local response. The September 11 attacks thus not only provided a stress test for the way the nation's homeland defense systems operated. It also created a case for testing how political institutions—especially the presidency and Congress—respond to sudden shocks to the political and policy systems. The stress test revealed critical problems in the nation's homeland security system. The intelligence community proved too fragmented and disjointed to assemble and digest the evidence it had collected. The intelligence system had not only collected information about many of the attack's elements, including flight training by suspicious individuals. It had also discovered that top al Qaeda officials were traveling broadly. Intercepted "chatter" warned of some impending event. The bureaucratic barriers between the intelligence organizations—the FBI, CIA, and NSA, in particular—prevented the needed coordination. First responders stunned everyone with their bravery, but the systems in which they worked showed other problems of coordination. Each new event, from anthrax to the shoe bomber, revealed unexpected vulnerabilities that, in turn, require further attention.

The shocks strained the system and revealed its vulnerabilities. The September 11 attacks, coupled with the anthrax attacks, revealed that the costs of failing to identify and solve the coordination problems in the nation's homeland defense could be extremely serious. To a degree never before seen in American politics, elected officials at all levels called for better coordination among all the terrorism prevention and response units. But as we shall see in the next chapter, the first step—improving coordination among the bureaucratic agencies—proved a large hurdle indeed.

C h a p t e r

3

The Federal
Bureaucracy Responds

IN THE AFTERMATH OF THE SEPTEMBER II ATTACKS, federal officials urgently debated about how to respond. Everyone agreed that the attacks revealed deep and fundamental problems with the federal bureaucracy, and everyone agreed they had to be fixed. At the same time, however, experienced Washington hands know that moving the bureaucracy requires uncommon patience and great skill. Bureaucratic reform has often seemed a case of an irresistible force meeting an immovable object. Even with the unparalleled shock of the terrorist attacks, no one knew quite how the bureaucratic landscape would change.

The first steps came in President Bush's address to a joint session of Congress just nine days after the attacks. It was an evening of both profound solemnity and great celebration. For the first time since the attacks, all of the branches of government gathered under one roof—the justices of the Supreme Court, both houses of Congress, and President Bush. Conspicuously absent was Vice President Dick Cheney, carefully hidden at a "secure undisclosed location" away from Washington, in case the terrorists struck again. To thunderous applause, cheers, and whistles, Bush's wife, Laura, came into the chamber, followed by New York Governor George E. Pataki, New York City Mayor Rudolph W. Giuliani, a New York City police officer, and a New York fire chief. Bush's speech proved one of his best ever. The audience interrupted him thirty-two times with applause. "We will rebuild New York City," he pledged.[1]

At the end of his speech, Bush held up the shield of police officer George Howard, who died trying to rescue people trapped in the World Trade Center. The president spoke solemnly, "It is my reminder of lives that ended and a task that does not end."[2] He pledged a multifront campaign against terrorism and demanded that the government of Afghanistan, where al Qaeda was based, hand over the group's leaders. He also announced the creation of a new White House office devoted to homeland security and headed by Pennsylvania Governor Tom Ridge. Bush had known Ridge for years and had seriously considered naming him as his vice presidential running mate. Ridge had military experience and was one of the nation's most respected Republican governors. Bush pledged to bring him into the White House and create a new homeland defense strategy. Ridge's job, according to one homeland security expert, was to find "someone who can connect those dots."[3]

Bush had quickly sorted through competing options. In the face of the co-ordination problems that the September 11 attacks revealed, some members of Congress pressed him to create a new cabinet department devoted to homeland security. Such a department, they believed, ought to bring together all of the government's agencies devoted to homeland security. In particular, they said, the government needed the new department in order to consolidate the government's intelligence operations, which had failed to detect the terrorists' plot. Bush, however, resisted. Having run for office as a conservative dedicated to restraining the growth of government, he did not want to create a new entity that would undoubtedly become one of the government's largest organizations. He argued instead for a more limited new organization: a White House office, headed by Ridge and supported by a small staff, whose job it would be to coordinate the government's existing agencies. That, the president hoped, would help strengthen the government's capacity without creating a large new agency that went against his small-government principles. Everyone agreed on the need for better coordination of the nation's homeland security functions. But there was wide disagreement on how best to ensure it.

THE ORGANIZATIONAL CHALLENGE

For years before the attacks, experts had been studying the risks of terrorism, and they had repeatedly pointed to the government's great problem in coordinating its many agencies to work effectively in concert. For decades, different agencies had managed different parts of the intelligence function. The FBI dealt with domestic threats; the CIA, with foreign threats. The NSA gathered electronic intelligence from spy satellites and intercepted cell phone calls. The Defense Department had a separate intelligence operation, with each of the armed forces running its own intelligence shop. So did the State Department and the Secret Service. The president's National Security Council (NSC) was ultimately responsible for digesting all the information and presenting it to the president, but sometimes the agencies did not share sufficient information with the NSC or with each other to permit possible threats to become clear. Each agency worked hard to defend its turf. That made it hard for a clear, integrated picture of possible threats to emerge, and gaps often developed in intelligence gathering and analysis.

Still other federal agencies were in charge of safeguarding the nation's borders. The Coast Guard was in charge of guarding the waters off the U.S. coastline. The Immigration and Naturalization Service (now called the Bureau of Citizenship and Immigration Services)—a part of the Justice Department, although much of its work abroad was done through State Department consulates—was responsible for keeping dangerous people out of the country, and the Customs Service (in the Transportation Department) was responsible for keeping out dangerous goods. The Department of Agriculture's Food and Safety Inspection Service and Animal and Plant Health Inspection Service were charged with protecting the nation from the importation of harmful food, plants, and animals. The National Park Service kept an eye on the land and coastal territory that was part of national parks and seashores. Within the Department of Health and Human Services, the Centers for Disease Control and Prevention (CDC) monitored possible risks from disease and bioterrorism. The Nuclear Regulatory Commission monitored the security of nuclear power plants, but the Department of Energy safeguarded former nuclear weapons production facilities and the nation's stockpiles of weapons and weapons-grade plutonium.

Different agencies were responsible for providing aid in case of a terrorist attack. The Department of Health and Human Services housed several agencies (including the CDC, the Public Health Service, and the National Institutes of Health or NIH) charged with responding to public health emergencies. The Federal Emergency Management Agency (FEMA) responded to natural disasters, such as hurricanes, tornadoes, and floods. But its workers also were trained—and in turn trained state and local officials—to deal with terrorism-related disasters such as building collapses. The Department of Transportation's Federal Highway Administration (FHA) and FAA had highly trained crews ready in case of damage to critical infrastructure. The Environmental Protection Agency (EPA) had specialists on radiological and chemical threats.

In sum, the federal government had extraordinary expertise, but that expertise was highly compartmentalized. Threats—especially terrorism threats—demanded carefully integrated intelligence and response, but as the September 11 attacks showed, such coordination could prove lacking at the most critical moments. Coordination is the central element of all bureaucracies, and problems of coordination are their most persistent pathology. Management expert Chester I. Barnard put it best, "Organization, simple or complex, is always an impersonal system of coordinated human efforts."[4] The September 11 attacks proved how difficult it is to pull expertise together and create a secure system or seamless response. As one reporter explained,

> To get an idea of the number of federal agencies potentially involved in counterterror efforts, just trace what the terrorists were doing in the days before the attack of September 11. As they set out for America months before the attacks, the CIA presumably was trying to recruit some of their Al Qaeda comrades as informants; the State Department, to persuade Arab governments to arrest them; the Treasury, to freeze their bank accounts; the military, to plan a raid on their Afghan training camps. As they came into the country, Customs checked

their baggage; Immigration checked their names against a watch list. As they lived among us, the FBI tried to track them down. As they boarded their chosen planes, the Federal Aviation Administration was trying to keep airport and airline security up to date on the latest threats.

They still got through.[5]

Complexity and Coordination

Better coordination, experts agreed, was what the government most needed to prevent future attacks and to improve the nation's ability to respond should attacks occur. But a staggering range and number of agencies are involved. Figure 3.1 shows how the twenty-two federal agencies moved into the new Department of Homeland Security were organized. One glance at the figure shows why coordination—connecting the dots—has proved so difficult. Which agencies should be linked? How? Homeland security includes so many different agencies performing so many different functions, that drawing clear lines is difficult. Figuring out how to make all the agencies work together is far harder. As journalist Sydney J. Freedberg Jr. observed, "The U.S. government was just not designed with terrorists in mind."[6]

Bureaucratic Autonomy

Not only are the players numerous and varied, but all have their own ideas about what they ought to do and how they ought to do it. The political scientist Herbert Emmerich argued long ago that "[t]here is a persistent, universal drive in the executive establishment for freedom from managerial control and policy direction." In fact, "The desire for autonomy characterizes the operating administrations and bureaus."[7] Managers, like most other people, want flexibility in how they do their jobs. Over time, most of the federal government's managers have come to know far more about their work than almost anyone else. As a result, they believe strongly that they know best how to accomplish their respective missions. Bureaucrats tend to have a strong self-interest in promoting their autonomy and frequently fight off any efforts that smell of control. In the meantime, many of these same bureaucrats have a strong professional and personal interest in working hard to respond to policymakers.[8] It is one thing for the government to build strong bureaucracies possessing great expertise. It is quite another for each of these bureaucracies to peer past its own boundaries for ways to cooperate with others.

The intricacy of homeland security, however, leaves government officials little choice but to rely heavily on government bureaucrats. Unfortunately, these mixed desires make it difficult for policymakers to manage the conflicting incentives of bureaucratic autonomy and responsiveness. Every effort at cooperation inevitably

Figure 3.1 Homeland Security Department

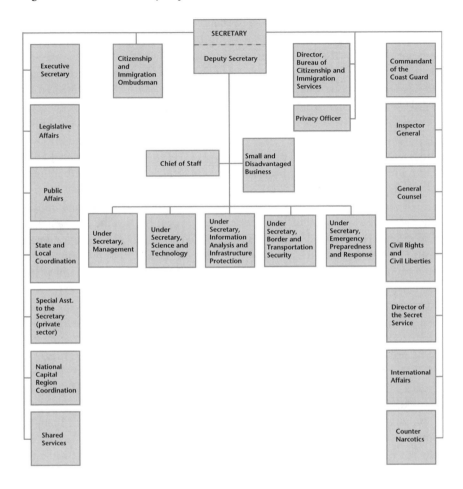

requires each side to give a bit and, most importantly, to surrender a bit of the very autonomy that managers fight so to protect. In truth, cooperation is risky. It requires managers to step out of their relatively protected enclaves. It can put programs, prerogatives, and budgets at risk. Managers often find it easier and safer to retreat from complex problems, burrow into their agencies behind tall barriers of rules and procedures, and shrink away from coordination. In particular, such forces made it hard for the intelligence agencies to share what information they had collected. No single agency had a full picture, but if carefully assembled, their individual pieces would have given senior government officials intriguing hints about the disaster that al Qaeda operatives had planned.

Mission Conflicts

The long history of different, sometimes conflicting, missions among the various intelligence agencies made it hard for them to share what information they had collected. In the years leading up to the September 11 attacks, both the CIA and the FBI collected information on al Qaeda operatives. The CIA tracked them in other countries, along with many other foreign threats. The FBI identified possible al Qaeda members inside the United States, but at the same time its agents remained focused on the bureau's traditional mission of tracking and capturing criminals such as bank robbers. Each agency had other missions in addition to the detection and prevention of terrorist threats. As former attorney general Dick Thornburgh testified before a congressional committee, "The FBI can't connect all the dots if it doesn't have all the dots in the first place."[9]

The same conditions characterized other areas. In border security, for example, the INS tracked persons entering and leaving the country, but the Customs Service reviewed materials coming in. One agency monitored plants, and another scrutinized food products. As securing the safety of the food supply became more important after September 11, this fragmentation created numerous hurdles.

Individual agencies pursued what they viewed as the most important issues. These competing and conflicting missions often did not overlap. Agencies did not see things the same way. Intelligence, as a result, slipped through the cracks. "It's no surprise that the FBI and CIA don't cooperate. We haven't wanted them to—until now," explained homeland security specialist Gregory F. Treverton.[10]

Each agency had a core mission separate from the core missions of the other agencies; none focused solely on homeland security. Each had other important missions for which it was responsible. To bend the mission to accommodate the coordination demands of homeland security risked undermining an agency's other—and, in the minds of many agency managers, more important—missions. No one wanted to put the nation at risk, but everyone wanted to make sure that they accomplished their core tasks as well.

Indeed, homeland security was not a new mission to replace old ones but a new mission added to existing ones. Agencies found themselves heavily pressed to do all of what they used to do and at the same time solve the new and often fuzzy problems of homeland security. Worries about new terrorist attacks caused senior Coast Guard commanders to shift many of their assets—fast cutters, small patrol boats, and a substantial number of forces—to homeland security duties. But no one suggested for a moment that the Coast Guard should not respond, just as quickly and effectively, to boaters in trouble or to sailors lost at sea. Nor did anyone suggest curtailing the war on drugs, in which the Coast Guard also plays a major role. Keeping up with these crosscutting responsibilities strained the Coast Guard. For instance, in Pittsburgh, where the agency helps control traffic on the busy Ohio River, homeland security activities grew from only 10 percent to 50 percent of the Coast Guard's workload after the September 11 attacks.[11] Meanwhile, the time the Coast Guard spent on drug interdiction declined by 60 percent from 1998 to 2002. Time invested in preventing foreign encroachment on American fishing territory and enforcing fishing laws shrank 38 percent. As the General Accounting Office (GAO) concluded, "The Coast Guard faces fundamental challenges in being able to accomplish all of its new homeland security responsibilities, while rebuilding capacity in other missions to pre–September 11th levels."[12]

Different Cultures

More than just meshing different agency missions, coordination also requires integrating the very different organizational cultures of these agencies. Although some analysts have questioned whether "organizational culture" is anything more than a mushy term with uncertain meaning, anyone who has spent any time working in an organization knows that each one is different. Each has its own unwritten rules; its own lore about who really makes the key decisions, how to dress, how best to spin a new idea to win approval, and in truth, whether new ideas are even welcomed. Workers at Disney theme parks go through intensive training to learn how to treat all visitors as "guests." Elsewhere, the service offices of some companies provide nothing like "service." In every organization, as Anne M. Khademian contends in her insightful book *Working with Culture,* the people working there share understandings about how things get done, and those common understandings define an organization's culture.[13]

Meshing organizations with very different cultures can pose vast challenges. It is one thing to try to integrate border security. It is quite another to link Coast Guard members, who are part of a uniformed military service, with immigration control officials, who work at desks and in airport terminals. The culture of the Animal and Plant Health Inspection Service is also different. It employs a "Beagle Brigade," dogs with green vests whose job it is to sniff piles of luggage arriving on international flights in search of contraband plant products that could carry dangerous organisms into the country. Different cultures cause people to think differently about how to do their jobs and even about what jobs are most important to do.

Existing cultures can also blind employees to homeland security issues and make it difficult to incorporate homeland security into existing missions. The FBI, for example, faced a massive task in working homeland security into its traditional missions, such as combating organized crime, tracking white-collar criminals, and protecting civil rights. The FBI not only lived by the watchwords, "We always get our man (or woman)." Its agents also received intensive training in how to carefully and deliberately build a case before arresting a suspect and then collecting evidence to ensure a conviction. FBI officials were convinced that no law enforcement agency in the world was its better and that terrorism on U.S. territory was its turf.

This cultural mindset created barriers to collaborating with other agencies, especially the CIA. Terrorism specialist Michael O'Hanlon put it like this:

> Suppose that the CIA generates information from its deep intelligence sources, such as infiltrators, for example. The FBI might want to acquire the information and to use it to arrest potential terrorists. Later, it might then want to use that information in a court to convict the terrorists. If the CIA shares the information, however, it might put its sources at risk; it might lose an infiltrator who took years to burrow into a terrorist organization and gain the trust of its leaders. A public trial in court might also reveal capabilities, electronic and human, that the terrorists did not know the United States had. Thus, the CIA's sharing of information with the FBI might jeopardize its ability to collect intelligence and perhaps track down terrorist ringleaders. On the other hand, the CIA's penchant for secrecy could make it harder for the FBI to convict terrorists and put them behind bars. Each agency had long had strong incentives to do its own business in its own way. These fundamental differences in organizational culture undermined the ability of analysts to connect the dots in the days before the September 11 attacks, and afterward they still proved extremely difficult to bridge.[14]

The FBI's culture was part cop and part lawyer. Terrorism presented a stark challenge to its traditional culture. For this agency, homeland security was more about detecting and preventing terrorist attacks than about finding and arresting the perpetrators. It put far more focus on quick actions in advance than methodical actions after the fact. The CIA's culture was part research and part intrigue. The two cultures did not mesh well. An official at the Customs Service, founded in 1789 to catch people trying to bring goods into the country illegally to avoid paying the import duty, put it bluntly: "You don't throw away centuries of culture and history overnight."[15]

Gaps: Distance and Technology

Even when agencies and their leaders wanted to coordinate closely, physical barriers could intervene. FBI headquarters is on Pennsylvania Avenue, just a few blocks from the White House, but the CIA is miles away and across the Potomac River, in Langley, Virginia. The NSA is even farther away, in Fort Meade, Maryland, midway between Washington and Baltimore. The NIH is in Bethesda, Maryland. The Public Health Service is nearby, but the CDC is based in Atlanta, Georgia. The Department of Health and Human Services oversees the NIH, PHS, and CDC, and its offices are just a few blocks from the Capitol in downtown Washington. Long distances also separate the federal government's emergency response agencies. The Federal Emergency Management Agency is in downtown Washington, but its Fire Administration is more than an hour's drive away, in Emmitsburg, Maryland.

Of course, technological advances, including secure teleconferences, make it possible for officials of different agencies to share information and counsel. Physical distance, however, contributes to the difficulty of bridging different agency cultures. At the Department of Health and Human Services, for example, Secretary Tommy Thompson announced a new "One HHS" strategy that was meant to integrate the department's agencies into a single, well-functioning operation. The goal, according to one HHS report, was to "help create 'One-HHS' that looks at our programs from the citizens' perspective and closes the performance gap by providing seamless and integrated services to our constituents."[16] However, officials in some of HHS's far-flung operations, especially in drug approval and public health, had long been accustomed to operating with great independence. They wondered whether Thompson's plan made sense, what its object was, and whether he and his senior staff could understand the technical complexity of their work. In short, they showed all the classic signs of agency officials seeking to protect and increase their autonomy.

Managing technology can further frustrate coordination. There is no better symbol for the technical barriers to securing better coordination than the FBI's Trilogy system. One of the organization's problems was that its information systems continued to run largely on paper instead of electronic systems, and the paper simply did not flow fast enough to the right people to help key officials make critical decisions before September 11. After the attacks, the FBI accelerated development of its computer information system, called Trilogy, but the costs of the project quickly soared. "Unfortunately, Trilogy has become a large disaster," complained Sen. Judd Gregg, R-N.H., chairman of the subcommittee overseeing the bureau's budget. "FBI software and hardware contracts for Trilogy have essentially become gold-plated. The cost is soaring. The schedule is out of control." New systems for conducting criminal background checks and checking fingerprints ran into long delays and cost overruns. In the trial of Oklahoma City bomber Timothy McVeigh, the agency failed to turn some documents over to his lawyers because they had been lost. An FBI agent who spied for the Russians, Robert Hanssen, used the agency's own computer system to check whether anyone inside the FBI had discovered that he was passing secrets.[17]

The Trilogy project had three parts: upgrading the desktop computers throughout the agency, upgrading the data networks and servers, and loading investigative programs onto the Web. For years, antiquated computer systems had crippled the ability of field agents to track information. When the FBI launched Trilogy, many of its computers were more than eight years old, and replacement parts for some of them were no longer available. Many of the computers did not even allow the use of a mouse to navigate the screen. When agents wanted to search for evidence, they often could do little more than conduct simple word searches of text documents. In the pre–September 11 days the bureau struggled to manage forty-two different data systems, none of which was adequate. Because the databases were not electronically linked, every time an agent needed to search for information, he or she had to check each system.[18] It was also impossible to connect the different databases. When the FBI tried to upgrade the computers in its field offices, it found that the offices lacked fiber optic cables to provide network access; after the computers were installed, there was insufficient software to run them. Pressed for funds, the bureau planned to reduce funding for Trilogy, and that infuriated some Democrats. "The FBI continues to operate with a 20th century computer system as terrorists are engaging in 21st century cyberwarfare," said Sen. Charles E. Schumer, D-N.Y.[19] Even after September 11, applicants submitting information for security checks had to find a typewriter to complete the forms and then mail them; online filing was not available.

High personnel turnover in the information technology area also plagued the FBI. Top officials sometimes were not supportive of technology upgrades. Moreover, external pressures, especially from members of Congress, whipsawed the agency among competing priorities. An anonymous source recalled a conversation with former director Louis Freeh. The bureau director was frustrated and complained that "every time there was a sound bite by a powerful congressman or senator saying, 'We need to devote more attention to car jacking,' for example, someone in the bureau would call a press conference and transfer 400 agents. Although [there were] voices crying in the wild saying we need a much more sophisticated and secure [technology] system, the bureau was always being pulled in different directions."[20]

Congressional Jurisdictions

Some of the most difficult homeland security coordination problems flowed from congressional decisions. The complicated homeland security mix was the product of organizational design decisions that had accumulated, quite literally, over hundreds of years. As Kenneth A. Shepsle and Mark S. Bonchek put it, "The bureaucracy is created by Congress and sustained by Congress."[21] Congress establishes agencies and the programs they manage, passes the budgets that they spend, oversees their work, and proposes fixes to agencies and programs that work poorly. The president might be the "chief executive," but most agencies interact much more frequently with Congress and especially with the committees and subcommittees that oversee them.

The structures of executive branch agencies reflect the complexity of the congressional committee system. Early in the long debate over how to strengthen the nation's homeland security system, analysts counted eighty-eight congressional committees and subcommittees that had jurisdiction over some aspect of homeland security. Any reorganization of homeland security agencies would also require a reorganization of Congress—or strong action by agency administrators to overcome the splintering worsened by Congress's own fragmented structure. Sen.

Pat Roberts, R-Kan., pointed to the problem of accommodating "old bulls [on Capitol Hill] who don't want their turf scratched." He continued, "How on earth do you give one person cabinet status and budget authority over the eighty federal agencies that are now involved without involving the Congress?" As one Republican aide described the debate over restructuring the nation's homeland security agencies, "There's no question this will be one of the most complicated undertakings of legislation in a long time."[22]

In *The Accountable Juggler,* Beryl A. Radin explores the art of leading a federal agency. She explains that American political institutions, by design, fragment power to prevent concentrated power from developing anywhere. Moreover, "The internal structure of Congress mirrors the larger fragmentation of political power."[23] The nation's Founders were sensitive to the risks posed by power concentrated in the hands of a king and determined to guard the new nation against them. Some scholars have wondered since if they overcompensated, creating a system too prone to fragmentation and hence ineffective in tackling tough problems requiring coordinated action.

Indeed, this is one of the central dilemmas of homeland security: at its core, homeland security requires coordination, but the government agencies that must cooperate find themselves pulled in different directions by the fragmented institutions—especially Congress—that oversee them. Because of its sheer size and sprawl, James L. Sundquist explains, "the bureaucracy appears to those on Capitol Hill to be beyond anyone's control."[24] Members of Congress see their job as making good policy. Their oversight of the bureaucracy requires a tight rein, and within Congress, that leads to irresistible pressures for fragmentation. The connect-the-dots arguments made in response to September 11 required just the reverse, and that set the stage for an epic battle over control of a hypersensitive issue.

Structured Organizations, Networked Threats

Complicating the federal government's strategy was a bureaucratic form of "asymmetry." The government organized its agencies along traditional lines of hierarchy and authority. Each agency had its own job, and each person within each agency had an assigned task. To work, bureaucracy requires that people do their jobs and not meddle in the jobs of others, or things risk falling through the cracks. Moreover, *government* bureaucracy actually requires agency managers to do *only* their respective jobs. Bureaucracies operate under authority delegated from Congress. As a safeguard, Congress delegates authority narrowly, and federal law prohibits spending government cash for anything other than the purposes for which it was appropriated. Bureaucracies in general, and government bureaucracies in particular, work within a model that assumes that careful definition of roles and responsibilities is the most effective way of operating.

By contrast, terrorists tend to operate in a distinctly nonbureaucratic fashion. In a RAND analysis of the possibility of technology-based attacks, what distinguishes terrorism "as a form of conflict is the networked organizational structure of its practitioners—with many groups actually being leaderless—and the suppleness in their ability to come together quickly in swarming attacks."[25] Thus, the asymmetry lies not only in differences of power and strategy involving razor-sharp attacks against broad and powerful forces. It also lies in differences of organization, with the attackers organized primarily in loose networks, and the defense structured principally in formal bureaucracies. In fact, the RAND analysts concluded, "the more a terrorist network takes the form of a multi-hub 'spider's web' design, with multiple centers and peripheries, the more redundant and resilient it will be—and the harder to defeat."[26] Moreover, the more terrorists organize through networks, the more important coordination among the defenders becomes.

FIRST STEPS

When he began settling into his White House office in September 2001, Tom Ridge found himself surrounded by problems. The nation remained edgy. Intelligence analysts warned that al Qaeda might launch more attacks. Anthrax suddenly became a big threat. Everyone concluded that the key intelligence agencies had to do a much better job of sharing information, but each quickly circled the wagons to prevent the new Office of Homeland Security—and the other agencies—from encroaching on its power and autonomy. Ridge found himself with perhaps the toughest job in government after the president's—a prime spot of West Wing real estate near Bush's Oval Office, but with sweeping challenges to address and few resources. He had an office with no bureaucracy and a mandate to make the entire country safe.

To further complicate his job, Ridge faced immediate tussles with Congress, some of whose members insisted that they wanted to pass a law authorizing his new office and setting out Ridge's powers. "If he is not granted a certain amount of authority, he is not going to be very effective," an aide to one Democratic member of Congress said.[27] What members of Congress left unsaid was that if Ridge remained a presidential appointee without congressional confirmation, they would have little control over his operations. If they could pass legislation authorizing the office, setting out its powers, gaining the right to confirm him in office, and controlling the office's budget, they could dramatically shift the balance of power. Many members of Congress saw this as one of the biggest new initiatives in decades, and they wanted to ensure that they could control its direction. Bush turned them down, saying through his spokesman that the president did not need congressional action to do what was required. On October 8, 2001, less than a month after the September 11 attacks, Bush signed an executive order creating Ridge's office.[28]

Ridge stepped into his job as another in a long line of White House "czars" charged with coordinating government policy on important problems. The history of such czars—from faith-based social services to energy conservation to drugs—has not generally been happy. They start their jobs with strong presidential support, high-level public attention, and a broad mandate. But they typically find, as Ridge quickly did, that without power over agency budgets and the authority to issue orders to federal employees, they have little more than a bully pulpit. Ridge could call attention to homeland security issues, try to get agency officials to work together, and talk to the American people about how to reduce the risk of terrorism. But he could not order anyone to do anything. Ridge could encourage the FBI and CIA to share intelligence better, but he could not force them to do so, and he lacked any leverage but the power of persuasion in the cause. Faced with entrenched bureaucracies, all of which had strong missions and stronger procedures, Ridge found his power limited. As one observer pointed out, Bush's executive order establishing the Office of Homeland Security uses the word "coordinate" more than thirty times. It does not use "command" or "control" even once.[29] Members of Congress were convinced that Ridge needed legislative authorization to do his job. Bush feared that that would lead to congressional meddling. At least at first, Bush won.

Then came a fierce debate about how best to prevent a repeat of the September 11 hijackings. With lives on the line, no one wanted to be blamed for another attack. The White House and many members of Congress raced forward with their own airport security plans. Everyone agreed on the need for a dramatic change in the screening of passengers and their baggage. The FAA immediately put into place new rules that prohibited carrying a wide variety of potentially dangerous items onto airplanes. Passengers found waits at airport screening equipment growing from minutes to as much as two hours. When they passed through the machines, screeners confiscated anything that might be used to harm flight crews, from the small files on nail clippers (flyers could keep the clippers, but screeners snapped off the nail files and put them into a secured box) to small pocketknives. The government later modified the rules to permit nail files but prohibit metal scissors, to allow eyelash curlers but prohibit cattle prods and martial arts weapons. Just to make sure everyone got the message, the government put out a long list of banned items, from the obvious (hand grenades and blackjacks) to the less-obvious (chlorine for pools and turpentine, which could be used to disable flight crews or to start fires).

More difficult was the question of who ought to do the screening. Before September 11, screening was the responsibility of the airlines, with private security companies enforcing federal rules. Everyone agreed that the responsibility could no longer rest with the airlines, and disturbing stories had accumulated about the performance of some of the private companies doing the work. Investigators found that one company, Argenbreit Security, had hired dozens of screeners who had criminal records. Low pay—often lower than what fast-food workers in the terminals earned—and poor working conditions led to massive turnover, as high as 400 percent per year at St. Louis's Lambert Airport and 375 percent at Atlanta's Hartsfield International Airport. Moreover, in tests, screeners missed twice as many mock weapons as European screeners did.[30] Because the airlines paid for the system, it was part of their operating costs. With the threat of hijacking low and pressures on profits great, airlines had little incentive to spend more money or make the process more difficult for their passengers—until September 11.

A consensus quickly emerged among the president's advisers and members of Congress that the screeners ought to be under federal control. But should the screeners be federal employees or private employees under far stricter regulation?

The last thing the Bush administration wanted, after pledging to shrink the size of government, was to create a new federal bureaucracy. Federal officials counted 429 airports across the nation, and they estimated that they needed a force of more than forty thousand screeners. The administration argued that private companies, under tough federal standards, could do the job, as was the case across Europe. "My approach gives the government the flexibility it needs to assemble a skilled and disciplined screening workforce," Bush said in his October 27, 2001, weekly radio address.[31]

Senators had a different idea. They were convinced that only a full federal takeover could eliminate the problems of the existing private system. Air travel had collapsed, with people afraid to get on planes or discouraged by long lines at security gates, and the Senate was convinced that travelers would never return to the air in large numbers without the strong assurance that would come from full federalization. Sen. John McCain, R-Ariz., put it plainly: "The American people do not have the confidence they need to have to fly on an airplane."[32] A privatized system would not restore confidence, senators concluded, and without fresh confidence in aviation, the economy would be crippled. By a rare unanimous vote of 100–0, the Senate approved a fully federalized airport screening system, a plan to deploy new air marshals to provide added security aboard planes, and new requirements for the installation of secure cockpit doors.

Members of the House, especially those in the Republican majority, sided with the president. They wanted to restore the confidence of the flying public, but they also fought hard against expanding federal employment. But the Senate refused to budge, and the Thanksgiving holiday weekend, the busiest flying days of the year, was drawing near. Bush wanted to keep the employees private, but he wanted the bill even more. He signaled that he was willing to compromise, the House agreed, and Congress passed a bill close to the Senate version. It created a new Transportation Security Administration (TSA), within the Department of Transportation, to hire airport screeners and enhance airline security. In a signing ceremony on the Monday before Thanksgiving, November 2001, Bush and congressional leaders went across the river to Ronald Reagan National Airport. They all agreed that the new TSA team would make it safe to fly again. Bush pointed to provisions that he likened to practices in the private sector, which would make it easy to remove screeners who performed poorly. Democrats praised the new federal agency. Of course, it would take the new TSA months to get up to speed and to hire new federal employees. The changes would make no difference for the upcoming holiday weekend. But federal officials hoped that the bill would prove an important symbol, at a symbolically important travel time, of the nation's resolve to enhance security. Ultimately, it had two effects. There were no new terrorist attacks, and travelers began returning to the air. The new TSA scarcely solved the problem, however. Determining how best to balance travelers' security with convenience became a perpetual balancing act.

THE RESTRUCTURING STRUGGLE

Despite the passage of the transportation security bill, Democrats in Congress continued to press for a stronger congressional role in homeland security. They did not like the way that President Bush had seized the initiative, and they feared that his efforts would shift power away from Capitol Hill to the White House. They continued to argue for a full-scale department of homeland security. Congressional Democrats also pressed for the creation of an independent panel to investigate the September 11 attacks, what could have been done to prevent them, and what the nation needed to do to increase its security. In presenting the Democrats' case, Senate Majority Leader Tom Daschle of South Dakota said that the events demanded "a greater degree of public scrutiny, of public involvement, of public understanding."[33]

Administration officials, including Vice President Cheney, countered that further terrorist attacks were virtually certain and said that the nation needed to join with the president to enhance security. His implication: Now was not the time to engage in what he tried to present as a side battle over a new department. Now was not the time to divert attention away from preparing for the future to examine what had happened in the past.

The sparring ended abruptly in June 2002 with the explosive testimony of Minneapolis FBI agent Coleen Rowley before the Senate Judiciary Committee. She complained that top FBI officials had not responded quickly to hints that possible terrorists were training to fly planes. They had refused requests for a search warrant to examine the computer of the man that some federal agents suspected of being the "twentieth hijacker," Zacarias Moussaoui. (Many federal investigators later concluded that he was likely not directly involved in the September 11 plot, but that he might have been positioned to help conduct a future round of attacks.) As senators listened intently, Rowley detailed her worries about Moussaoui before September 11 and her frustration in working her way through the FBI's layers of authority to obtain approval for the search. She criticized the

Agent Coleen Rowley, from the FBI's Minneapolis field office, testifies before the Senate Judiciary Committee on June 6, 2002, about the office's investigation of Zacarias Moussaoui, whom officials charged with conspiring with the September 11 hijackers. In a thirteen-page memo, she detailed roadblocks headquarters officials set up to block the investigation of Moussaoui's activities. Later that evening, in a speech in which he proposed the creation of a new department of homeland security, President Bush told the nation that he expected top government officials to treat such inquiries seriously.

FBI's culture, which had made it impossible to communicate her concerns to the right officials. "There's a certain pecking order, and it's real strong," Rowley said. In the FBI's way of doing things, agents were not to go over the heads of their immediate supervisors, and working her way up the chain of command proved daunting. Headquarters officials often second-guessed the decisions of field agents. "Seven to nine levels is really ridiculous," Rowley told the senators.[34]

Bush and his advisers smelled big trouble. Rowley's testimony suggested that, if senior FBI officials had better processed the information they had had, they might have been able to detect and prevent the attacks. More fundamentally, the testimony illustrated the bigger problems of coordination for homeland security—and it raised large questions about whether the president's plan for Ridge's Office of Homeland Security had gone far enough. Bush sensed that Rowley's testimony would provide support for the Democrats' efforts to create a homeland security department. He decided to steal their thunder—and to ensure that if there were going to be a new department it would be on his terms, not theirs.

In Bush's new plan, twenty-two federal agencies with homeland security responsibilities would be combined into a single new department, with a secretary, structure, and budget subject to congressional approval. Bush told the nation, "As we have learned more about the plans and capabilities of the terrorist network, we have concluded that our government must be reorganized to deal more effectively with the new threats of the twenty-first century." To counter the fears of conservatives and balance his own earlier objections, he explained that the reason for creating the new department was not to increase the size of government, "but to increase its focus and effectiveness."[35] Its budget would start at $37.5 billion, and the new department would have 160,000 employees, more than any other department except Defense and Veterans Affairs.

Congressional leaders in both houses and in both parties welcomed the plan. It effectively deflated the pressure for a sweeping investigation of the September 11 attacks, an investigation that the Republicans wanted to avoid. It also stopped short of the much broader reorganization that some wanted but which many Republicans opposed, under which the CIA and FBI would both have been swept into the new department.

There was grand irony in the immediate political success of Bush's proposal. Coleen Rowley's testimony stirred up serious concerns about the effectiveness of the nation's intelligence services and their ability to share information effectively. The proposal for a homeland security department short-circuited questions about the intelligence community without reorganizing it. To be sure, launching the new department would be sufficiently difficult and complex without including the FBI and CIA as well. "What I'm proposing tonight is the most extensive reorganization of the federal government since the 1940's," Bush said in his June speech.[36] Bush's plan avoided the toughest problems while providing a large connect-the-dots symbol.

In many ways, the administration's plan was the most complicated restructuring of the federal government ever proposed. Besides bringing together the aforementioned twenty-two federal agencies and a vast number of employees, it proposed increasing these agencies' focus on homeland security without sacrificing any of their existing missions. The department would include the major federal agencies responsible for border security and emergency response but leave out many others with homeland security responsibilities, notably those responsible for intelligence collection and interpretation (Table 3.1). Intelligence officials inside the Bush administration argued successfully that with the terrorist threat continuing, it was no time to upset existing expertise. The restructuring therefore concentrated on the government's border security, airline security, infrastructure protection, and emergency response agencies.

In the act creating the department, Congress resolved the question of which agencies ought to be included with relative speed. The House quickly passed the bill in July 2002. But tensions sharpened in the Senate about the rules for

Table 3.1 The Department of Homeland Security

What's *in* the department

(Agencies moved to the new department. Departments in which agencies were previously located are in parentheses)

Border and Transportation Security	• U.S. Customs Service (Treasury) • Bureau of Citizenship and Immigration Services (formerly Immigration and Naturalization Service; part transferred from Justice, part remains) • Federal Protective Service (General Services Administration) • Transportation Security Administration (Transportation) • Federal Law Enforcement Training Center (Treasury) • Animal and Plant Health Inspection Service (part transferred from Agriculture, part remains) • Office for Domestic Preparedness (Justice)
Emergency Preparedness and Response	• Federal Emergency Management Agency (formerly independent agency) • Strategic National Stockpile and the National Disaster Medical System (Health and Human Services) • Nuclear Incident Response Team (Energy) • Domestic Emergency Support Teams (Justice) • National Domestic Preparedness Office (FBI)
Information Analysis and Infrastructure Protection	• Critical Infrastructures Office (Commerce) • Federal Computer Incident Response Center (General Service Administration) • National Communications System (Defense) • National Infrastructure Protection Center (FBI) • Energy Security and Assurance Program (Energy)
Science and Technology	• Chemical, Biological, and Radiological Countermeasures Program (Energy) • Environmental Measures Laboratory (Energy) • National Biological Warfare Defense Analysis Center (Defense) • Plum Island Animal Disease Center (Agriculture)
Citizenship and Immigration Services	• Bureau of Citizenship and Immigration Services (part transferred from Justice Department)
Coast Guard (Transportation)	
Secret Service (Treasury)	

staffing the new department. The Bush administration, backed by key Republican senators, wanted greater flexibility in hiring and firing employees and wanted to limit employees' collective bargaining rights. Bush said he needed additional flexibility to act promptly in times of national emergency. Bobby Harnage, then the head of one of the government's largest unions, countered, "We see the administration's use of 'flexibility' as a code word for denial of due process to federal employees." The Senate version, he charged, would make it too

What's *not* in the department (A sample of major agencies with homeland security responsibilities that were not included in the restructuring)	
Central Intelligence Agency	
National Security Agency	
Department of Agriculture	• Animal and Plant Health Inspection Service • Food Safety and Inspection Service
Department of Defense	• Defense Intelligence Agency • Northern Command (charged with defense of American territory)
Department of Health and Human Services	• National Institutes of Health • Centers for Disease Control
Department of the Interior	• National Park Service Police • Bureau of Land Management Police
Department of Justice	• Federal Bureau of Investigation
Department of State	• Bureau of Consular Affairs (including issuance of visas)
Department of Transportation	• Federal Aviation Administration
Department of Treasury	• Bureau of Alcohol, Tobacco, Firearms, and Explosives • Customs

easy for the administration to crack down on whistle blowers. The administration's plan "means nothing less than gutting the civil service merit system and busting employee unions," Harnage said.[37] Senate Majority Leader Daschle supported the union's position, but Sen. Phil Gramm, R-Texas, staged a filibuster to block passage of anything but the president's plan. The homeland security bill remained in legislative limbo until after the November 2002 midterm congressional elections.

Those elections, however, produced stunning gains for congressional Republicans, who kept control of the House and won control of the Senate in the new Congress that convened in January 2003. Senate Democrats were stung, and they quickly worked out a compromise on the personnel issues that had held up the bill. The department's senior officials would have great flexibility in pay, promotions, job classification, performance appraisals, discipline, firing, and collective bargaining. Union officials won some modest protections, but on the whole, the Bush position won. The changes were, in fact, not quite as radical as they seemed. The Internal Revenue Service (IRS) and the FAA's air-traffic control system had been operating for years under similarly flexible rules. But this was a huge federal restructuring involving a giant new department. Union leaders and their Democratic supporters wanted to avoid further erosion of their power. Bush and the Republicans were just as determined to avoid creating a big new group of federal employees represented by Democratic-leaning unions. The Republicans' surprise victories in the 2002 midterm elections quickly resolved both the political and the policy questions. As he signed the bill, Bush praised the new department, which he said would ensure "that our efforts to defend this country are comprehensive and united."[38]

The new department faced daunting tasks, from hiring and training air marshals and integrating the vast new airport screener workforce to developing new strategies for screening checked baggage and securing the nation's ports. It was a truly huge challenge. Tom Ridge, named as secretary of the new department, not only had to get the department geared up and functional—he had to do it while ensuring that terrorists could not exploit cracks in the system during its startup. He and his management team had to pull together twenty-two different federal agencies, bridge their cultures, and integrate their missions. He had to deal with a Congress whose organization—and oversight—had changed little with the creation of the new department and whose fragmentation could tear the department apart. Ridge and his top advisers moved into a new headquarters on Nebraska Avenue, three miles from the White House and twice as far from Capitol Hill. The new department's constituent agencies and workers remained in their existing locations, with headquarters scattered around Washington, and the majority of its employees—the airport screeners—were dispersed across the country. The logistical challenges alone were huge.

So, too, was balancing the new department's relationship with the public. As the symbol of the nation's fresh attention to homeland security, the department needed to be firm and effective—quickly. It needed to do everything humanly possible to prevent a repeat of the September 11 attacks or the anthrax attacks. That required tough action to screen passengers and luggage at airports and containers arriving aboard ships from abroad, as well as careful scrutiny of people trying to enter the country. At the same time, the department had to be careful not to make harried travelers even more worried. The attacks knocked several airlines into bankruptcy, and the tourist industry around the world suffered. Citizens worried about threats to civil rights and civil liberties. Somehow, the new department had to determine how best to balance security and service. More of one often meant less of the other. Tighter airport screening could mean longer waits to board airplanes, but efforts to speed up transit through airports could leave vulnerable cracks that terrorists could exploit. The central task of the department's new leaders was to determine, somehow, the best way to balance these competing goals—without drawing political attacks for making the wrong choices.

THE BATTLE OVER BOUNDARIES

At the very least, the new Department of Homeland Security was a symbol to re-assure the American public. Left largely untouched was the biggest problem that the September 11 attacks revealed: the great difficulty the nation's intelligence services, especially the CIA and FBI, had in sharing and digesting collected intel-ligence. Almost two years after the September 11 attacks, one reporter concluded that "even though they both need their relationship to work, they have such dif-ferent approaches to life that they remain worlds apart. In fact, they speak such different languages that they can barely even communicate." The cultures are hugely different. FBI agents tend to focus on specific things that can lead to iden-tifying suspects and making arrests. The bureau's culture rewards individual achievement, especially in putting criminals behind bars. By contrast, the CIA's employees tend to be more informal and place greater importance on developing relationships. "It's not that [FBI agents and CIA officers] don't like each other, but they're really different people," explained one former CIA analyst. "They have a hard time communicating."[39]

The fundamentally different cultures that made it difficult for the two agen-cies to connect the dots before September 11 changed little in the first years after the attacks. Changing organizational culture is hard, especially when the risks are great and when preexisting missions (such as catching bank robbers and finding spies) continue to be important. Moreover, the CIA-FBI problems are multiplied by the boundaries traditionally drawn between their operations, with the CIA re-sponsible for foreign threats and the FBI charged with defending against domes-tic ones. The Terrorist Threat Integration Center established by President Bush to be the repository for all information related to terrorism helped bring CIA and FBI employees into the same room, but it also generated new turf battles.

Some analysts compared the communication problems of the CIA and FBI to the ones that John Gray discussed in his bestseller *Men Are from Mars, Women Are from Venus*.[40] Some insiders despaired that either side would ever be able to push its culture aside to build a strong working partnership with the other. Other ex-perts suggested that it might take a decade or more, during which time the nation would remain vulnerable to attacks. One sixteen-year CIA veteran observed, "I don't think the domestic al Qaeda is worried about [how to coordinate with] the foreign al Qaeda."[41] And some in Washington suggested that bridging the cultures might prove impossible and that integrating intelligence might require the creation of a new agency. They looked to Britain's famous security intelligence agency, MI-5, which has substantially greater powers than either the CIA or the FBI. Created in 1909 to help Great Britain protect its ports from German espionage, MI-5 has long had the responsibility of assessing all threats against the country, regardless of their source. With no history of separating domestic from foreign threats, MI-5 has never suffered from rivalries such as those between the CIA and the FBI. Of course, pushing aside the FBI and CIA to create a new agency would create an epic bureaucratic turf battle, and Washington officials continued to search for other solutions. The one option not on the table was bringing the two agencies into the new Department of Homeland Security, which now had responsibility for connecting all the dots, except for the very ones that proved most troublesome before September 11.

Beyond the intelligence questions, the new Department of Homeland Security struggled to define its mission and just what "homeland security" meant. Just which problems were within its province, and which ones were not? Given the substantial—and justified—criticism that the lack of coordination had increased American vulnerability, the instinct of the department's leaders was to be inclusive. If a problem *might* be a homeland security problem, then they would act on it accordingly. However, that instinct sometimes led to "mission creep." Intelligence analysts studied the Internet and concluded that a determined hacker could infiltrate the system, flood it with e-mails, and cripple transmissions. Given the nation's increasing dependence on the Internet for everything from commerce to communication, crashing it could have devastating consequences. Indeed, several attempts in 2003 showed just how serious the damage could be. The Department of Homeland Security therefore took on Internet security as one of its concerns. In short order, however, its concern about Internet-based terrorists spilled over to an initiative designed to help protect children from pornographers, child prostitution rings, and other predators who operated in cyberspace. In announcing "Operation Predator," Secretary Ridge said, "Harming a child in any manner or form is a despicable, despicable thing."[42] While that was unquestionably true, its connection to homeland security stumped many observers.

These two tales—the difficulty of coordinating intelligence and the difficulty of defining the department's boundaries—provide powerful evidence for a fundamental truth in the homeland security debate. While much of the discussion centered on the mission—what needed to be done to protect the nation, and how best to do it—the most important decisions flowed more from political than from mission-based motives. To say that is not to impugn the motives of those involved in the debates. Those discussions were long and difficult, and they produced few clear answers. The lack of any real, black-and-white answers left decision makers trying to see subtle differences in shades of gray. With little else to guide them, they had to sort out questions according to the values they shared, and that made the key decisions political, in the most essential sense of the word. Everything about restructuring the nation's homeland defense system revolved around trade-offs: of safety versus service, of protection versus freedom, of presidential leadership versus congressional oversight. Given the high stakes and even higher uncertainty, decision makers had to rely on their best sense of what to do.

The September 11 attacks subjected the national government to a brutal stress test. Congress and the president responded in very different ways. Each sought both a symbol to show its determination to prevent a recurrence of the attacks and a response to ensure that, in fact, future attacks were prevented. Both sought a strategy to make the nation's homeland defense far stronger. And officials in both branches struggled to ensure that, no matter what the strategy, they would retain a measure of control over what had suddenly become the most important policy issue in Washington.

Bush fell back on the presidential instinct to solve problems by focusing on people and relationships. He was not interested in a large restructuring of the nation's homeland security organizations, because he believed that that would only enmesh his efforts in ongoing turf wars and frustrate his ability to act. Members of Congress, by contrast, focused on structures, budgets, control, and oversight. Congress passes laws; it does not carry them out. For Congress to get traction on the issue, it had to think and act legislatively; and laws meant money, organization, and power.

Events, especially FBI agent Rowley's testimony, which was based on a memo she wrote about the issue, forced Bush to move toward the congressional position, but as he did so, he ensured that he got a bill to his liking. The Democrats held up final action on the homeland security bill in the hope that the November 2002 elections would strengthen their hand. When the elections put both houses of Congress in Republican hands, Democrats beat a hasty retreat and gave Bush most of what he wanted. But they hardly gave up on the homeland security issue. Several key strategists believed that the Democrats could make Bush vulnerable on the issue during the 2004 presidential campaign, especially with respect to coordinating intelligence, but at least in the Homeland Security Department's first years, Bush and the Republicans held the upper hand.

Coordination—connecting the dots—was thus as much a political as an operational issue, one over which the Republicans and Democrats tussled. It provoked constant turf battles among powerful bureaucracies. Dramatically upended by the September 11 attacks, the nation's political system struggled to right itself. At the core, though, one question remained more important than any other: Can there be executive branch coordination as long as legislative fragmentation remains? As with everything else the federal government does, the nation's system of separation of powers remained one of the most important touchstones.

At the operational level, the difficulties of getting such a vast array of federal agencies to coordinate carefully created a huge hurdle for ensuring and maintaining coordination. Multiple and conflicting missions distracted agency managers. Different cultures made it hard for agency officials to synchronize their operations. And no agency wanted to surrender its autonomy to others. Put together, these forces magnified the problems of coordination. They also increased the difficulty of sustaining effective coordination over the long haul. As the painful memories surrounding September 11 began to fade, the old instincts reemerged and pulled the agencies back into their old patterns. Despite the creation of the new department, there were already signs that pressures for backsliding were building, even as the demands for coordination grew.

4

State and Local Struggles

"ALL POLITICS IS LOCAL," former House Speaker Tip O'Neill once famously wrote.[1] To that we can add that all homeland security, at its core, is also local. The battle in Washington over creating the new Department of Homeland Security seized headlines. Yet any terrorist attack is, first and foremost, a local event: Every plane crash, explosion, or report of an illness, fire, or other problem requires a local response. The first workers to arrive on the scene are local firefighters, police officers, emergency technicians, and public health experts, not officials from the FBI or CIA.

On both the local and national level, few countries have invested more than Israel in trying to stop terrorist attacks during the Palestinian *intifada,* and the nation's security officials have prevented much bloodshed. Nevertheless, terrorists too often get through to detonate bombs on buses and around marketplaces. After a suicide bomber killed sixteen people at a hotel in Netanya in 2002, the town's mayor said that it was impossible to prevent terrorist attacks. "This is a city that can be infiltrated from many different directions," Mayor Miriam Feyerberg sadly explained.[2] Local first responders—those who first bring aid to those in trouble—raced to the scene.

Even though no security system is foolproof, for any U.S. public official to suggest anything less than complete protection—as Netanya's Feyerberg did in Israel—presents serious political problems. To admit publicly that citizens are at risk opens the door to charges that not everything that could be done has been done. The practical reality, however, is that full protection is impossible and that resolute terrorists can find a way to inflict damage. Thus, an effective homeland security system must include not only the kind of preventative efforts that preoccupied the Washington debate over the Department of Homeland Security, but also a strategy for managing the consequences of any attacks that do occur, and that job is fundamentally a job for local government.

A second fact that defines the role local governments play is that local officials learn of a terrorist attack in the same way that they learn about other emergencies, and they tend to respond in the same way. Someone calls 911 and reports a problem, and the dispatcher sends help. As was the case on the morning of September 11, sometimes the dispatchers need to send massive help. In New York City, two hundred fire units—half the city's force—responded to the World Trade Center, and the Pentagon disaster occupied all of the firefighters on duty in Arlington County. For the emergency teams it did not matter whether terrorists or something else had started the fires. When the alarms rang out across New York City, all that mattered to firefighters was that the Trade Center towers were engulfed in a massive fire and that people, including their brother firefighters (as the firefighters refer to each other), needed help. Whether sparked by terrorism or an accidental plane crash, a boiler explosion or a short circuit, fires are fires. Firefighters and other emergency responders jump into their equipment and roll to the scene. They leave it to investigators to piece together the causes later. For the first crews on the scene, the cause does not matter. Trained to fight fires, they size up the problem and put their training to work. Emergencies are emergencies.

The same is true of terrorist attacks that work through the public health system. The first signs of how widespread the effects of an anthrax attack could be came when postal workers began coming down with mysterious respiratory illnesses. One postal worker, Thomas Morris, worked at the Brentwood mail processing facility in the District of Columbia, which had handled the anthrax-laced letter sent to Senator Daschle's office. On a Sunday morning, he called 911 to say, "I'm having difficulty, and just to move any distance I feel like I'm gonna pass out. My breathing is labored, my chest feels constricted. I am getting air, but I, to get up and walk, what have you, feels like I just might pass out if I stay up too long." His doctor had taken a culture, but the doctor had not gotten back to Morris with the results. "The doctor thought that it was just a virus or something so we went with that, and I was taking Tylenol for the achiness," Morris told the 911 operator. But then he had started to vomit, a telltale sign of advancing anthrax, and he called for help. Fourteen hours later he was dead.[3]

Other postal workers at the same facility also came down with aches, pains, and symptoms similar to Morris's. What separated those who lived from those who died was the care they received from their physicians. Did the symptoms cause the doctor to consider the possibility of anthrax and prescribe Cipro, a common antibiotic that is almost always effective in countering anthrax if taken early enough? If the doctor guessed wrong and assumed it was simply a case of flu, the medication might be too late. Once the disease advances and spreads through the lungs, it is difficult to counter and death often results. For the physician, however, the symptoms—aches, pains, a raspy throat, and some congestion—match those of a host of diseases, many of which respond well to Tylenol. It would be overkill—and because of Cipro's possible side effects, dangerous—to prescribe the drug to everyone who presents flulike symptoms. Physicians have to be skilled in telling the common flu from the very uncommon—and very dangerous—symptoms of anthrax.

On November 6, 2001, biohazard workers moved into the Hart Senate Office Building in Washington, D.C. Officials closed the building, treated its employees, and worked for months to decontaminate it. The building reopened three months later, after a cleanup that cost millions of dollars. In February 2004, the cleanup experts returned to Capitol Hill when a mailroom employee discovered the deadly poison ricin next door in the Dirksen Senate Office Building.

These problems put heavy stress on first responders. Terrorist attacks typically start with common events that play out in uncommon fashion—fires, explosions, sniffles, stomach distress, skin irritations. The job of firefighters is to put out fires and rescue victim, regardless of how the fires started, who started them, or who the victims are. It does not matter to physicians whether terrorists or a chance exposure to a dangerous fungus on a farm sickened their patients. Their job is to treat them.

Thus, on one level, terrorist attacks are larger versions of what such frontline workers deal with all the time. On another level, however, the implications can explode on a far greater scale than first responders are accustomed to managing. Terrorist attacks can present problems totally unlike the ones faced by emergency workers every day. The September 11 attacks swamped the capacity of the New York Fire Department (FDNY), which is widely regarded as the world's best. Not only can the scale be larger, but analysts have warned about the risks of sophisticated terrorist attacks involving biological and nuclear materials. Firefighters could arrive on the scene of a fire to discover that terrorists had laced the area with lethal radioactive, chemical, or biological materials. Therefore, responses to terrorist attacks must fundamentally involve local officials, in ways that are both very similar and completely unlike anything they may have seen before.

THE DRAGON FIGHTERS RESPOND TO THE TERRORIST ATTACK

Fire Captain Jay Jonas worked out of Chinatown, on Manhattan's Lower East Side. Over the years, Jonas had carefully studied high-rise fires, and he was one of the department's most highly skilled experts. On the morning of September 11, Jonas and the other five members of Ladder 6 watched black smoke rise above Lower Manhattan. The alarm came in, and they jumped aboard their rig—christened "The Chinatown Dragon Fighters"—and sped the twenty blocks to the World Trade Center in just three minutes. Along the way, they caught sight of the flames roaring near the top of the North Tower, and they all knew it would be the worst fire they had ever faced.[4]

As one of the FDNY's leading experts on high-rise blazes, Jonas had quite literally written the department's book on rescuing people from them. When he and his Dragon Fighters arrived at the base of the North Tower, they quickly surveyed the scene and donned their gear—110 pounds of it, ranging from rope and air packs to special crowbars and protective equipment. American Airlines flight 11 had hit the building at about the ninety-second floor, igniting its jet fuel in a massive fireball and knocking out most of the building's elevators. The Dragon Fighters knew that victims were trapped near the crash site and that there was only one way to reach them, by climbing the stairs. And they knew they might need all their equipment. So they began the long and difficult climb up the narrow stairwells.

Along the way, they stopped twice to help other firefighters struggling with chest pains. Civilians were passing them heading down. They paused on floor twenty-seven to count heads. Jonas was worried to find two of his Dragon Fighters were missing, but a quick search found them gasping for breath one floor below. He decided to gather everyone in the lobby of the twenty-seventh floor for a breather. As they tried to summon more strength for the next stage of the ascent, they were stunned not only to hear but also to feel a tremendous concussion. They did not know it at the time, but it was the collapse of the South Tower, which had been hit by the second plane.

For Jonas, the situation was difficult to assess. He had no information about the South Tower or, indeed, about what faced him on the higher floors of the North Tower. The firefighters' radios had provided spotty communication at best, and he had not received any reports from the commanders in the lobby. The

Dragon Fighters found themselves on their own. The men from Ladder 6 knew that people were dying above them, and firefighters have always prided themselves on pushing into tough conditions where others feared to go. But Jonas saw that the stream of civilians moving down the stairwell had slowed to a small trickle. His knowledge of high-rise building fires told him that the North Tower was in serious trouble. He took on himself the authority to order the Dragon Fighters to evacuate.

On the way back down, they encountered a woman about sixty years old, in bad shape—obviously in pain and having great difficulty moving. Her feet were swollen and she was gasping for breath. One of the men put her arms around his neck and began guiding her down the stairs. The crew learned that her name was Josephine Harris. She was a bookkeeper for the Port Authority who had been working on the seventy-third floor when the first plane exploded above her. A grandmother from the Bushwick section of Brooklyn, she had somehow made it down more than fifty floors but could barely move any farther.

The radio, which had been silent, suddenly crackled with an order from the commanders to evacuate the North Tower. It was clear that the building might soon collapse, as the South Tower had already. The Dragon Fighters had little time and faced a tough choice. If they left Josephine Harris behind, they could move much more quickly and improve their own odds, though she would certainly die. If they carried her down the stairs, the building might collapse before they could reach safety. For the men of Ladder 6, there was no choice. They were trained to save people in trouble, and they had doggedly climbed up the stairs of the North Tower to rescue as many people as possible. They had found just one survivor to rescue and were determined to help her, slowly and painfully, down the stairs.

They moved Josephine Harris down to the fifth floor, but she could barely move. "Stop," she begged. "Leave me alone. I can't go any farther. Stop." The firefighters decided that they would have to carry her. Jonas started looking for an office chair to which they could strap her, but it was too late. They began to feel the building shake and the floors ripple. The floors above them started to pancake, "and there were these huge explosions—I mean huge, gigantic explosions," firefighter Sal D'Agostino remembered. "It was like a train going two inches away from your head: bang-bang, bang-bang, bang-bang," said his colleague, Bill Butler. D'Agostino added, "I remember thinking—this is how I go. This is it, this is it, this is it." Jonas later said, "The tower came down like a peeling banana, and it peeled around us."[5]

The collapse tossed the men around and turned the stairwell black. D'Agostino struggled to get a deep breath only to discover that he could not. One of the members of Ladder 6 found that he could not talk because his mouth had been packed with the pulverized remains of the building. Jonas started a roll call, and miraculously, he found all of his men alive, scattered among several floors of the bent and twisted stairwell. Suddenly, a figure popped up out of the dust. It was Josephine Harris, still carrying her purse.

As Jonas surveyed the scene, he discovered that sixteen people had been nearby when the building collapsed. Fourteen were still alive, but they did not know just where they were, what things were like outside, or how to escape. Over the radios they heard reports of fires throughout the World Trade Center complex, and Jonas heard explosions around him. He worried that more debris would collapse underneath or on top of them. But the Dragon Fighters continued to work to get Harris and the other survivors out. One rigged a harness to secure her and lowered her one half of a landing. But at that point they were stuck. They saw no means of escape through the debris.

Jonas found a radio that a chief, killed in the collapse, had been carrying. He sent out a Mayday call and was relieved to hear the voices of friends saying, "I'm coming to get you." The trick was finding out where they were. Jonas radioed that the group was in Tower 1, Stairwell B, scattered between the second and fifth floors. Another firefighter on the frequency sent a puzzled reply, "Where's the North Tower?" It simply was gone, crumbled around them. There was no more Stairwell B because there was no more North Tower. Amid the collapse, it seemed a miracle that they had stopped where they had. Anyone below them had died in the rubble of the collapse, and those still above them were caught in the debris. Somehow the stairwell had proven a lucky lifeboat. From the sound of fires crackling around them, however, they knew they were not yet safe. Josephine Harris turned to one of the men and said, "I'm cold." One of the firefighters bundled her in his coat—and then realized that if she was cold, it must be from outside air. One of the men used his Halligan, a special crowbar, to punch a hole through the wall to the outside. Once almost at the bottom of the North Tower, deep inside a stairwell, they discovered they were atop the pile of debris. The crew also found that they were in great danger, because the other buildings in the World Trade Center complex were fiercely burning all around them.

Rescuers from Ladder 43 found them and began easing the men of Ladder 6 out of the stairwell. The Dragon Fighters edged their way across the debris, and the Ladder 43 firefighters brought out Harris. Somehow, all of the Dragon Fighters escaped, along with the woman they had worked so hard to rescue. The men from Ladder 6 decided that she had been their guardian angel. If they had not slowed to help her, they would have made their way farther down the stairwell, or even outside the tower, only to have it collapse on top of them. Their rig, parked just outside the building, had been crushed down to its axles, and only the tip of a tail remained of the brass dragons that rode on the truck.

The news media proclaimed Jay Jonas and his team heroes. Television news-magazine shows featured Josephine Harris and the men of Ladder 6, and each broadcast the gripping tale of their survival. But Jonas reminded audiences of the deaths of fellow firefighters and said, "This is what all the guys—343 of our friends—this is what they were doing, too." He added, "We weren't doing anything special. We weren't doing anything differently than they did. These guys who were killed were all heroes."

In fact, the men of Ladder 6 were doing the same things that thousands of other firefighters and police officers were doing that morning. Mindless of the threats to their own safety, they rushed into the burning towers, intent on saving as many innocent individuals as they could. What mattered was that they were doing their jobs—not whether the fires had been started by a terrorist attack or by an accidental plane crash. High atop two of the world's tallest buildings people were in trouble, and the first responders were determined to help.

Acts of terrorism put special burdens on the first-response system. But they begin as so many other emergencies do: the alarm goes off, and teams like Ladder 6 jump into their trucks to respond.

GAPS IN THE SYSTEM

Emergency planners have long recommended that local officials follow an "all-risk" strategy: build a strong, basic capacity for local emergency response and deploy that capacity when needed to deal with problems, regardless of what caused them—storms, accidents, or terrorist attacks.[6] There are different ways of preparing for terrorist attacks, but with modest luck these are rare events. No city can afford to create a special team devoted solely to terrorism. Moreover, as the men of Ladder 6 found, dealing with a building collapse requires the same fundamental techniques regardless of the cause. Effective response to terrorism depends on an effective first-response system that can handle a wide range of occurrences.

To be sure, it might not be necessary to send a fully equipped ladder company to respond to a traffic accident. Some communities have experimented with dispatching more mobile and lightly equipped crews to such events. On the other hand, as September 11 showed, even the best trained and equipped first responders can find themselves overwhelmed. Thus, an all-hazard approach might be too much for some emergencies and not enough for others. Still, the philosophy is the foundation for the nation's terrorist response system.

So, too, has been the principle of mutual aid. In catastrophic situations, local governments typically rely on mutual aid agreements with neighboring communities under which reinforcements can be brought in quickly. However, because of its enormous size and capacity, the FDNY had no formal mutual aid agreements with surrounding jurisdictions. When assistance from surrounding communities rolled in on the morning of September 11, it was poorly coordinated.

In other states, efforts to build such agreements have sometimes foundered in practice. For example, Texas had been trying to help governments build stronger mutual aid agreements for years, but the program repeatedly was derailed by a fundamental dilemma: If smaller communities joined larger communities in a regional approach, they sacrificed their right to separate funding. However, larger communities often would not guarantee that they would respond to problems in smaller towns for fear that serious events would overwhelm their own capacities. Yet if smaller communities decided to go it alone, they were not large enough to build the capacity they needed. It was a dilemma to which neither state nor local officials had a solution.[7]

The mutual aid problem underlined a broader problem that researchers found across the country: Local first responders could hold their own against the dangers they faced most often, but they were underequipped for responding to terrorist events. The seriousness of the problem varied widely. Following their own survey, researchers from the RAND Corporation found, "The majority of emergency responders feel vastly underprepared and underprotected for the consequences of chemical, biological, or radiological terrorist attacks." The problem was partly technical and partly simple uncertainty. Emergency workers "felt they did not know what they needed to protect against, what protection was appropriate and where to look for it."[8] Firefighters needed equipment that was lighter and easier to work in. Police officers needed better body armor and improved dashboard computers. All of the first responders needed better monitors to detect chemical, biological, and radiological hazards.

Everyone wanted better equipment, but local departments also needed better training and improved coordination. Some of the coordination problems were also technological. In New York, fire commanders often could not communicate with their teams because the concrete and steel in high-rise buildings blocked their radios. Firefighters often had little or no communication with police commanders. On the morning of September 11, the NYPD had helicopters circling the burning towers, but fire commanders received no reports from them on the condition of the burning buildings. Those watching the buildings on television had more information than did the fire commanders. In many communities around the country, police, fire, and emergency medical technicians use different radio frequencies and cannot communicate at the scene of a disaster. Emergency workers in one jurisdiction often have found it difficult or impossible to communicate with first responders in neighboring jurisdictions, or with officials at the state or the federal level.[9]

The same Texas officials who were stumped about how best to develop coordination between communities also struggled with such communication problems. The state had established three frequencies for local first responders to use to request aid. The Texas Forest Service had supplied fire departments with vehicles and ensured that each could receive at least one of these three frequencies. But the first-response teams instead tended to use their own limited-range radios, and too often drivers simply forgot to turn on their trucks' units designed for communication with neighboring jurisdictions. Larger jurisdictions were not part of the program; nor were other first responders such as police officers and emergency medical technicians. After carefully examining the program, one team of analysts concluded that "the puzzle of communication interoperability appears to be almost insurmountable."[10]

Another example of the difficulty of coordinating first responders occurred during the October 2001 anthrax scare. The mailroom supervisor of a large Wisconsin insurance company was worried about a suspicious package. He called 911, and the emergency dispatcher sent the fire department. When the firefighters arrived, they ordered everyone to move quickly outside and to strip to their underwear so that the firefighters could hose the workers down for decontamination. It was a chilly day—and a scary and unpleasant experience for the employees. About forty-five minutes into the event, someone finally decided that they ought to bring in public health officers, but when the public health official arrived, she was not allowed into the command trailer because she was not recognized as part of the first-response team. After more confusing conversation, the public health worker was finally allowed into the area but only under the direction of the fire chief, who was certainly well meaning but greatly uninformed about how best to treat the event. The public health official quickly discovered that the suspicious material was a liquid inside test tubes. Anthrax is a powder. Thus everyone went through a long and difficult ordeal for nothing, and the public health officer could have headed it off. But public health was not part of the first-response team, and the lack of coordination hindered handling the emergency properly.[11]

A 2003 Council on Foreign Relations study found that two years after September 11 "the United States remains dangerously ill prepared to handle a catastrophic attack on American soil." The council found that fire departments often could supply radios to just half of the firefighters on a shift and that only 10 percent of the nation's fire departments had the people and equipment to rescue people trapped in a building collapse. Police departments lacked the gear to protect their officers following an attack with weapons of mass destruction, and most states did not have adequate equipment, expertise, or capacity to test for biological or chemical attacks. "America's local emergency responders will always be the first to confront a terrorist incident and will play the central role in managing its immediate consequences," the CFR study observed. It concluded, however, that the first responders were "drastically underfunded" and "dangerously unprepared."[12]

New York City and Arlington County struggled mightily to deal with the fires and building collapses of September 11. By any measure, however, these communities were among the very best prepared in the country. In fact, the awful attacks occurred precisely where first responders were best prepared to limit injury and loss of life. They would have been far worse in many other communities.

Unfortunately, under close examination, even the best prepared communities showed dangerous gaps in equipment and training. First responders everywhere discovered that the coordination with neighboring communities was often weak. Some of the problems were technical, like an insufficient number of radios whose signals could penetrate concrete and steel and radios that shared frequencies with nearby towns. Some of the problems were political and bureaucratic, because just as was the case at the federal level, individual departments and local governments struggled to maintain their autonomy. Local officials often wanted to run their own departments in their own way, and the burdens of coordination usually meant they had to surrender some of their power to someone else. Most emergencies present fresh problems that demand new patterns of coordination, but established bureaucratic patterns often make that hard.

COORDINATION IN THEORY AND PRACTICE

Homeland security takes many of the traditional problems of organizational coordination, multiplies them enormously, and vastly raises the stakes for success and failure. It also introduces new elements that must somehow be incorporated with the old. Effective homeland security requires tailoring coordination to the special nature of homeland security problems, and each incident requires a response tailored to the special needs it presents.[13]

Both theorists and political leaders have traditionally relied on organizational structure to solve coordination problems. The traditional "scientific management" approach to public administration, first elaborated in the early twentieth century, lays out a clear prescription: Break down complex jobs into their component parts; structure those parts so that bureaucrats have the capacity to do hard things well and to do them well on a regular basis; and maintain the organization so that doing the complex well becomes predictable. For traditional public administration, coordination is thus a *structural problem* to be solved by *organizational design.* For political leaders, public organizations also have an important symbolic purpose. Creating, maintaining, and sometimes changing bureaucracies can send citizens signals about what leaders value and show that they are taking action on those values.[14]

The classic view of coordination through structure builds on Luther Gulick's work in *Papers on the Science of Administration.* Gulick laid out a fundamental model of organizational structure that is at once deceptively simple and remarkably prescient:

> Wherever many men are thus working together the best results are secured when there is a division of work among these men. The theory of organization, therefore, has to do with the structure of co-ordination imposed upon the work-division units of an enterprise. Hence it is not possible to determine how an activity is to be organized without, at the same time, considering how the work in question is to be divided. Work division is the foundation of organization; indeed, the reason for organization.[15]

In short, accomplishing tough jobs requires the division of work among workers. Gulick goes on to argue that organization requires dividing work and establishing coordination among the pieces. According to Gulick, there are four—and only four—ways of organizing: according to purpose (or function), process (or the way things are done), clientele (the individuals served), or place (the location being served). Organizational leaders must choose one—and only one—of the four.

Though his point might seem pedestrian, his arguments are in fact quite profound. Gulick argues boldly that a leader's strategic choices for organizing bureaucracies (and, by extension, preparing for homeland security) are limited to four. He also contends that none of the choices is ideal; each has its advantages and disadvantages. So leaders make the necessary choice of one alternative, with the knowledge that the choice brings clear benefits and certain costs.

Governments generally have chosen *organization by purpose and function*. It represents what people think government does—put out fires, arrest criminals, build roads, provide clean drinking water—and brings together the experts responsible for accomplishing such functions. Gulick concluded that organization by purpose and function was most often the best choice because "purpose is understandable by the entire personnel down to the last clerk and inspector."[16] The argument flowed from Frederick W. Taylor's pursuit of scientific management, his focus on division of labor, and his emphasis on organizing by function.[17] When organizations had a difficult time finding highly skilled people to accomplish difficult jobs, Taylor's answer was not to search for better workers but rather to change the job, focus it more carefully on a narrower set of skills, and increase the number of people who could accomplish it.[18]

By the time Gulick wrote his paper in 1937, generations of analysts had framed the basic management strategies. Their work, coupled with research into scientific management, had identified organization by function as the basic building block of organizations. Indeed, Gulick's paper was important not so much because it was a theoretical breakthrough but because it so cogently captured the best thinking at the time.

Gulick recognized that organization by function carries with it fundamental problems. For example, it is usually hard to divide work neatly. That inevitably creates gaps and overlaps, which produce service problems and inefficiencies. Organization by function also tends to strengthen top-down managers, whose job it is to define functions and allocate responsibilities. That can blind managers to citizens' views and to feedback from employees who could suggest important improvements. It also can create organizational tunnel vision, in which the mission—and only the mission—matters. It can insulate managers from other managers in other organizations. Ultimately, Gulick warns, it can drift "very easily into an attitude of complete independence from all other activities and even from democratic control itself."[19] Given these problems, why do leaders continue to choose a functional system? The answer is that it matches so well with government's mission and the way that citizens expect government to pursue it. Moreover, the other three strategies of organization bring their own, even more difficult, problems.

Obviously, deciding on the strategy for designing first-response organizations scarcely solves all of the problems. Nevertheless, as Christopher Hood has pointed out, when disasters occur, a common response is to suggest that "the problem (whatever it was) could have been averted if only there had been more co-ordination, better procedures, more planning and foresight, clearer assignment of authority, more general 'grip' on the part of experts, professionals, or managers." The typical solution is "to tighten up the rules and authority structures to prevent a recurrence."[20] That brings more pressure for more restructuring, and as a result, few organizational design strategies remain stable. But that has not prevented elected officials from resorting to structural solutions to complex problems, in part because of a deep-seated conviction that better structure will in fact produce better results and in part because restructuring produces a strong and visible symbol of action to hard problems, even if the new structures fail to solve the old problems and sometimes introduce new problems of their own.[21]

The debate on how best to solve these structural problems has been endless. Out of the debate, however, comes a clear message: coordination is a *contingent* problem, and what works best depends on the problem to be solved. What it is, how it works, and how best to create the solution depend on the nature of the issue, the nature of the organization, and the nature of its employees. Structures rarely adapt easily enough and quickly enough to meet the challenges that hard problems present. So the very strategies deployed to improve coordination often become the targets for critics when problems occur—and so the bureaucrats and managers seek to reorganize yet again.

Herbert Simon has proposed a different approach. Rather than seeking coordination through structure, Simon argues for *coordination through decision making,* which would allow decision makers to tailor strategies to specific events. Indeed, the problems that emerged in the response to September 11 powerfully reinforced Simon's argument about the need for contingent coordination. For example, New York City had long divided its public protection operations along the traditional functional lines of police and fire. The fire department did not want to adopt the police department's communication standards, and vice versa. These rivalries stymied the implementation of new coordination systems. Incident management was so centralized that when the World Trade Center buildings collapsed, they destroyed the operations grid that told fire commanders which crews were working where in which building, and it took hours to determine who was missing and where they might be found. The fire and police commanders did not share information, nor did they have the ability to coordinate their operations, so warnings from the police helicopter overhead never reached the fire commanders.

On the other hand, the Arlington County commanders had developed more finely tuned coordination mechanisms. They had recognized the potential gaps that a functionally based system could create during a disaster, and they worked in advance to bridge these gaps. Their response to the attack on the Pentagon represented the launch of pretested coordination plans, not an effort to rig a new coordination system on the spot.

The New York City effort, amid one of the largest and most complex emergency service crises any force anywhere has ever faced, was heroic by any standard. The Pentagon scene was far smaller and more manageable. But Gulick's analysis suggests why, at the core, coordination was so hard to manage in New York: It required the linkage of strong, functionally organized bureaucracies to solve a place-based problem. The more intense the crisis, the harder that coordination is to ensure. Gulick, in fact, wondered, "Are there limits to co-ordination? Is mankind capable of undertaking activities which though interrelated are beyond man's power of systemic co-ordination?"[22]

Public officials have tended to approach these questions by trying to design organizations, typically by function, to secure coordination. Such structural design has been useful—indeed, it would be hard to imagine a different first and basic step on which to build the system. But as terrorist events have shown, there are limits to the degree of coordination that organizational structure can achieve because the problems can be so huge and unpredictable. Many of the key coordination puzzles of homeland security, in fact, require nonstructural approaches, including interorganizational networks (such as mutual aid agreements among fire departments), improved information technology, and stronger political leadership. With these elements in place, first responders and officials are better able to adapt to the unpredictability of a specific emergency.

Simulations conducted by the federal government have proved just how hard it is to build effective networks for coordination. In May 2003, the Department of Homeland Security conducted a major exercise to test the system's response to a simulated dirty bomb detonation in Seattle and the pneumonic plague in Chicago. The exercise, christened "TOPOFF," for the "top officials" who were involved as key players, revealed serious coordination problems, especially in communication between federal and local officials. At one point local officials could not get the medical equipment they needed because no one knew which federal agency was responsible. One anonymous government official said, "The criticisms are among the worst I've ever heard."[23]

In political terms, restructuring was the natural and predictable response to September 11. In administrative terms, restructuring was a necessary but insufficient condition for improved coordination. Local officials, in fact, argued that if the nation wanted better coordination, it was going to take a lot more money.

MONEY

With every new terrorism scare or heightened alert, local governments face big costs for overtime. Experts have called for more investment in communication and protective equipment and laboratory testing, but the demands hit amid the worst state fiscal crises in fifty years. State and local officials recognized the need but said they could not meet it without federal help. Federal officials had their own budget problems, with swelling deficits and new costs for improving intelligence gathering. The debate is, of course, the eternal one in American federalism: Who ought to pay for what and what strings ought to be attached to the money that is distributed?

The problem in part flowed from the huge financial demands of the new homeland security challenge. It quickly became clear that some communities, especially New York and Washington, faced greater risks than others. Places with large ports and critical infrastructure, such as nuclear power plants, also confronted higher risks and higher costs. Not surprisingly, analysts said that whatever federal money was provided ought to go directly to the communities facing those higher risks and costs.

On the other hand, these analysts also argued that regardless of where citizens lived, the government ought to provide at least a minimum level of protection to all. Terrorist events can occur anywhere. Indeed, one of the anthrax deaths in 2001 was a ninety-four-year-old widow in a small Connecticut town. Another was in a Florida city. Both were far from the New York and Washington focus of terrorism worries. The cases made the point that terrorism would not necessarily focus on the big cities and that governments nationwide needed to provide a minimum level of protection to their citizens.

For state and local governments, the terrorist attacks presented both huge demands and an unusual opportunity—an opening of the policy window—in which they could try to win new federal support. State and local officials agreed that they needed help, but how much was anything but clear. There was no agreement on how assistance ought to be distributed. Should most money be focused on the areas that faced the biggest threat? How much money ought to be distributed to all governments, so that they could provide basic protection to all citizens? To what extent should the federal government rely on state and local governments' own assessments of where the money needed to go? And how much should be spent on goals defined by the federal government? "We're talking billions and billions, and this money ought to be spent according to national, minimum standards," argued former senator Warren B. Rudman, who chaired the Council on Foreign Relations homeland security task force. "Unless we get these standards in place, we're going to have money wasted."[24] State and local officials countered that they knew better than any federal official how to deal with their own police, fire, and other emergency services.

There is no way of knowing which threats are most likely. There is no way of knowing how much preparation is enough. State and local officials know that they need better equipment, and they know they want the federal government to pay for it. The debate is inherently muddy and the dollar costs are unknowable. That creates a potentially insatiable demand for federal cash and a huge temptation to turn federal support into pork barrel politics, with money distributed to meet the political objectives of members of Congress. The very uncertainty of the issue makes it hard to resolve, but the risks of failing to resolve it well are clear. As Jim Schwartz, director of Arlington County's emergency services, put it, "The real scare for me is down the road, when we have another incident, will we have done the best job by our citizens with these moneys?" [25]

State and local governments criticized the federal government for talking tough on terrorism but failing to write the checks. For their part, some federal officials had long criticized some state and local officials for failing to take emergency planning seriously enough. For example, a CNN reporter found that when the federal government raised the terrorism alert level in early 2003, "some cities say they are already at a high security level and don't anticipate many changes." And "many cities did nothing in response because they didn't have the resources or didn't feel they were in danger." [26] Federal officials worried as well that more federal money would simply buy more of the same, without any real improvement in homeland security. [27] As FEMA's inspector general pointed out, state management of federal emergency programs is often highly uneven:

> States often do not monitor and accurately report on [the grant's] financial and performance activities, States do not always make or close out projects in a timely manner, and financial status reports provided to FEMA are often incorrect or untimely. In addition, States do not always maintain adequate documentation to support their share of disaster costs and other financial requirements. Finally, States do not always have adequate practices to account for equipment purchased with Federal funds. FEMA needs to take the initiative to assist the States in developing reliable grant management systems. [28]

At the core of the problem are two issues. First, in both political and practical terms, America's historical tradition of local self-government has limited federal control of state and local policy. Local officials have resisted federal efforts to dictate what they can do and how they can do it. Second, even if the federal government wanted to prescribe uniform state and local action, it is technically difficult to set and enforce standards, especially for emergency services. Homeland security necessarily involves multiple federal agencies, complex partnerships with state and local governments, and intricate ties between the public and nongovernmental sectors. This complex structure multiplies objectives and responsibilities— what government seeks to do and who is charged with doing it.

Without baseline goals and standards, it is impossible to determine how much money ought to be spent on which programs. The problem of homeland security produces unending demands for money, no good way to know what the money is buying, and no way of knowing when to stop funding.[29] It is also woven deeply into the fabric of American federalism, in which it is impossible for any part of the federal system authoritatively to define objectives and measures for the other parts.

This turns the focus to a basic question of American federalism. Should state and local flexibility be encouraged, so that the states can indeed be "laboratories of democracy"?[30] Should the nation follow Alice Rivlin's prescription that the key to better government in a globalizing world is "restoring a cleaner division of responsibility between the states and the national government"?[31] And if each subnational government sets its own policy, how can we ensure adequate protection for problems that cross over the boundaries of state and local governments? How can we ensure a minimum floor of protection for citizens, wherever they live? Should the national government ensure a minimum level of preparedness and response for all citizens, with the federal government defining and financing it and with state and local governments implementing it? John Donahue has warned, "Enchanted by the advantages of state [government] autonomy, we are rushing to abandon the far greater advantages of a continent-scale common front with which to face the coming century's economic pressures." In fact, he contends, if we fail to assert common goals, "state boundaries may become fault lines along which the American commonwealth will fracture."[32] If one substitutes "homeland security" for "economic pressures," his argument is even more telling and persuasive.

American federalism does not demand uniformity on all fronts. But just as there are matters of individual rights and civil liberties on which Americans rightly expect equal treatment, Americans believe that the government ought to provide basic protection from the risks of terrorism. Americans will not accept variations in risk and safety based on the arbitrary security measures of the town through which they happen to be passing at a given time.

One question is whether the federal government wishes to supply more money. State and local officials complained for years after the 2001 attacks that promised federal cash was slow in arriving. On the question of how the federal government ought to channel its assistance, three alternatives emerged:

- *No-strings.* From time to time, the federal government has used "revenue sharing" and other no- (or few-) strings approaches to distributing aid. However, such programs have always encountered problems. With no or few strings, the federal government has no control over how state and local governments spend the money. That has inevitably produced some tales of misspending, with federal officials exclaiming, "They spent the money on what?!" Not surprisingly, state and local governments favor grants with few strings. Just as understandably, national officials resist such programs, especially when the federal budget is tight.

- *Block grants.* Since the 1970s, the federal government has created broad-purpose grants and distributed the money by formula. The programs, ranging from community development to job training, have given state and local officials broad discretion over how to spend the money, but they have typically required submission of a plan for federal approval and a follow-up audit of results. State and local officials have long argued that they know their needs best and that the federal government ought to minimize its control of their decisions. Federal officials, on the other hand, have been nervous about even this level of flexibility.

- *Categorical grants.* There is a long tradition of providing federal support for narrowly targeted purposes, such as buying improved protective equipment for firefighters or better radios for first responders. Federal officials tend to prefer such narrow grant programs because they guarantee how the money is spent. State and local officials dislike them not only because they dislike being told that they can spend the money on some projects but not others, but also because narrow categories can frustrate coordination. Local officials, for example, often need financial help to tie related systems together, and categorical grants can reinforce the bureaucratic boundaries that local officials are trying to cross.

Beyond the question of grant strategy is a fundamental question of intergovernmental power. If the federal government does supply more money, should it flow directly to local governments or to state governments with a requirement that most of the money pass through to local communities? Local governments, not surprisingly, resist having any of the money go to state governments. They worry that passing the money through the states would add one more level of control and soak up too much of the cash in an already underfunded program. State governments contend that the real work of homeland security requires much more coordination among communities and that, left to themselves, the communities are not likely to create coordinated programs. Only state-level planning, accompanied by a measure of state-level control, is likely to ensure coordination. Both sides have taken their arguments to Congress in a battle over money and control. But the disagreements between the state and local governments have made it harder to build consensus in Congress for any given strategy, and that in turn has slowed the financial pipeline.

Homeland security is a new challenge for state and local officials. It is one that requires new and innovative strategies for coordinating emergency response. At the same time, however, it has quickly come to be plagued by all the traditional frictions in the intergovernmental system: Who gets how much money, under how much control? Homeland security has become a new arena for playing out the old games.

NORMAL ORGANIZATIONS AND ABNORMAL EVENTS

For local governments, homeland security is certainly not a new mission. Given the traditional focus on "all hazards," local first responders have long been counted on to counter disasters of all kinds. They have worked hard to hone their response to fires and traffic accidents, bank robberies and heart attacks, plane crashes and public health emergencies. For firefighters rolling out on their way to a large fire and building collapse, it does not matter whether a terrorist bomb or a natural gas explosion sparked the event—except that the new age of terrorism injects a harsh note of uncertainty into any such event. Is one bombing likely to be followed quickly by another? Could the flames be laced with dangerous radioactive or chemical or biological threats? Is the event on a scale so large that it strains the ability of local officials to manage it?

For local officials, the challenge is to use conventional organizations—police, fire departments, emergency medical technicians, and public health systems—to respond to unconventional events. From one point of view, terrorist events can pose large, catastrophic consequences demanding incredible bravery from first responders. From another point of view, feats of bravery are routine for first responders. The very nature of their day-to-day work puts their lives on the line constantly. The great challenge is equipping these key workers to do their routine, if dangerous, work well—and, at the same time, preparing them to respond effectively to the unthinkable with the kind of bravery the Dragon Fighters showed on the morning of September 11.

The state and local role in homeland security focuses many of the issue's toughest dilemmas. It underlines the role the coordination must play in ensuring that critical problems do not fall through the cracks. It spotlights the difficulty that federal officials have in understanding state and local problems. It reveals deep-seated cracks in the relationships between many states and their local governments and, indeed, the many additional fissures that separate adjoining communities. Add to this the inevitable lure of transforming federal homeland security aid into pork-barrel politics. It is very hard for federal officials, administrators, or members of Congress to concentrate money in some jurisdictions while ignoring many others. It is easy—and correct—to make the case that terrorism is a threat that can occur anywhere, even if its threat is unquestionably higher in some areas.

As the immediate, horrific memories of a terrorist event recede, the old and deeply rooted instincts reemerge. The key players all believe in homeland security, but they have very different ideas of what it means and how it ought to apply to their communities. Homeland security depends on a strong system of emergency response. That system depends, in turn, on federalism and the robust structure of the nation's state and local governments. However, this richly textured system of federalism contains powerful incentives for fragmentation, and in the absence of an overpowering force to bridge the cracks in the intergovernmental system, those cracks are likely to reemerge. The result is backsliding away from the mandate for new coordination in homeland security that seemed so clear in the days after September 11. Homeland security has created a new playing field for the old games, and has increased the risk that the system's fragmentation will undermine the nation's emergency preparedness.

The Political Costs
of Managing Risk

TERRORISM IS AN ESPECIALLY nasty and difficult policy problem. No system can anticipate every challenge it can pose. Even a system that works 99.9 percent of the time still can allow one attempt in a thousand to sneak through the defenses, with devastating costs in both human lives and property damage. As a result, a realistic policy program cannot focus on completely preventing terrorism. It must focus on *reducing the odds* of a successful attack to the maximum extent possible and ensuring that the damage from any attack that does occur is minimized.

To do this, however, is extremely difficult. No official wants to suggest publicly that full protection is impossible or that even the smallest amount of risk is acceptable. At the same time, no public official could long survive the furor that would come from imposing the costs and restrictions required to truly bring the risk as low as theoretically possible. Yet policymakers face precisely this Catch-22 situation constantly. Much of regulatory policy is about balancing risks to the public's health and safety with the costs of complying with the rules. How much research should a pharmaceutical company be required to perform before the government allows a new drug on to the market? How safe is safe enough? How much should a company be required to invest in reducing air pollution? If the pollution kills or injures people, how much of the company's investment is appropriate for the human lives saved? Every year, the news media capture stories of people made sick or killed by food poisoned by bacteria. How much should government spend inspecting stockyards, farms, transportation systems, restaurants, and grocery stores to save those lives? What is the risk of mad cow disease—and how far should the government go in trying to prevent its spread? Accidents at railroad grade crossings—where roads cross train tracks—kill hundreds of people annually and cause approximately a billion dollars every year in damage.[1] Those accidents could be completely prevented by building an overpass at every such crossing, but that remedy would be extremely expensive.

Puzzles such as these recur throughout the system. They dominate the issue of homeland security. Terrorism presents a potential for catastrophic damage that seizes the public mind and dominates the media, making it particularly difficult to frame policy and to weigh the trade-off between risk and cost.

More protection usually requires higher costs. Some of the costs are financial, through investment in sophisticated new technology. Others might involve the relinquishing of some individual liberties, as we shall see in the next chapter. Some of the costs might come through the emphasis on homeland security over other policy goals that are sacrificed in the name of greater security. For example, no passenger staggering off a long intercontinental flight wants to suffer long delays to retrieve luggage, to answer questions about any goods being brought into the country, to go through passport control, or to answer a battery of immigration questions. Indeed, during the 1990s, the federal government's immigration and naturalization and customs agencies invested great effort to streamline this process for haggard travelers.

It might be possible to dramatically reduce the odds that terrorists could carry dangerous materials into the country through a blockade of the borders and hand searches of everyone and what they are carrying. But given the long, open border with Canada and the miles of unpatrolled shoreline, even that would not be enough. In dealing with homeland security, the public rhetoric usually revolves around government's commitment to protecting its citizens. However, the reality that policymakers face is a far more difficult question: How much is enough?

BALANCING RISKS

How can a system guard itself against events that are rare, unpredictable, and, when they do occur, very costly? For many analysts, the answer has long been *redundancy:* calculated overlaps to reduce the odds that any part in the system might fail. For example, in the space program, there are redundant computer systems to protect against system crashes. There are multiple checks on every component. Ground crews and the flight crew cross-check their work. Engineers have built redundancy into airliners. They conduct tests to ensure that two-engine planes can safely take off and land on just one, in case an engine fails at a critical time. They blast bird carcasses into engine cowlings and across the pilots' windshields to make sure these components can survive an impact. The landing gear has multiple tires, and the electronic systems have backups. Redundancy has been designed into each of these systems to minimize risks and maximize safety.

Experts have long accepted, even celebrated, such redundancy. In a famous 1969 article, Martin Landau argued that redundancy and overlap provide greater security and improved results. In fact, he concluded, such redundancy could actually be efficient because duplication reduced the odds of catastrophic losses.[2] Multiple programs, duplicative organizations, and overlap among them provide defense in depth—if one agency misses a problem, the odds of catching it improve if there is another whose jurisdiction overlaps. Some "waste," by Landau's argument, is not really waste at all but an insurance policy against disaster.

Critics, on the other hand, have long complained about the redundancy approach. It celebrates the advantages of duplication, but it does not provide a clear guide about just where duplication ought to be implemented, how much is enough, how much is too much, and how to tell the difference. Taken to its logical extreme, redundancy could prove little more than a justification for massive inefficiency. That is the case in spades for homeland security, where the threats by definition are uncertain and unpredictable and where, therefore, massive redundancy could theoretically be comforting. Redundancy as a basic operating procedure could provide an excuse for sloppy planning and the waste of scarce human and monetary resources.

Of course, resources are always limited. No one likes paying taxes. But no one wants to suffer the consequences of a terrorist attack either. Everyone would like protection, but no one really wants to pay. These cross-pressures limit the extent to which redundancy can plug gaps in the system. Moreover, if redundancies are random, they could actually open the door to well-planned attacks: terrorists could avoid the areas where the government has created defense in depth and seek the areas where defense is much thinner. That is precisely what the terrorists did on the morning of September 11. Government investigators now believe that the system designed to prevent gun-toting terrorists from hijacking planes and holding passengers hostage allowed terrorists using legal blades to kill the crews and crash the planes. That is the core of asymmetric attack: avoid the areas with high redundancy, identify gaps, and exploit them.

Homeland security is fundamentally different from most government programs because there is zero tolerance for mistakes. But other programs share this feature. Navy pilots landing on aircraft carriers, for instance, must get it just right. There are no overrun areas, as there are for ground landings, and there is no side-to-side margin. The same is true for the operation of nuclear power plants and of the space shuttle, where tiny problems have proven catastrophic. While no one wants to see errors in mailing Social Security checks or processing building permits, mistakes in those programs are rarely fatal. In high-risk, zero-tolerance-for-error programs, however, the system must work all the time.

In extensive writings about "high-reliability organizations," Todd LaPorte and his colleagues have crafted a theoretical approach to solve this problem. Their theory provides a foundation for understanding homeland security problems.[3] In a 2002 article about the management of zero error tolerance, George Frederickson and LaPorte contend that such complex systems can suffer two kinds of errors: false positives and false negatives. "False positives" are investments in efforts to prevent terrorism when there is no terrorist risk. In such cases, government can spend money and focus energies on solving problems that turn out not to be problems. Managers spend money but get nothing for their investment. On the other hand, some errors are "false negatives," cases in which managers fail to detect risks until catastrophes occur. Managers save the resources, but everyone suffers from the mistake. That was what happened on September 11, when the terrorists exploited loopholes in the system.

Ideally, of course, one minimizes both kinds of errors: resources wasted on situations that are not problems and problems that the system fails to detect. False negatives—problems that sneak through—have the potential for catastrophe, so public officials worry most about eliminating them. At the core of all of this, however, is a tough trade-off. Investing more in the system to reduce false negatives can impose big costs and inconveniences for little gain. For example, following the unsuccessful 2001 attempt to sabotage American Airlines flight 63 with a shoe bomb, airport travelers found themselves subject to far more extensive searches. Travelers got used to removing their shoes for x-ray inspection. Some shoe manufacturers put their design teams to work substituting "security friendly" plastic supports for metal ones. But the whole process confused many older travelers, and flyers complained that it was inconsistent from airport to airport and sometimes within the same airport. Experienced flyers often picked shoes they knew would not set off the alarms, only to be told to take off their shoes anyway. One executive complained that the screening rules are "often capricious." As a result, "It's difficult to predict when it's going to be an easy process." Another frequent flyer complained that he occasionally came upon a gate agent who seemed to suggest, "You'll do what I say or you're not going anywhere." On one flight, the flyer was pulled over for a random screening and groaned, "Oh, man." The agent brusquely told him, "Don't raise your voice. I can keep you from getting on that airplane." [4]

If someone managed to get through security without a full screening, or if someone tripped the alarm at an emergency exit, security officials would pull everyone back into the lobby and force them to undergo screening and x-rays of their carry-on baggage again. Pilots sometimes returned to the gates if a passenger made a poorly timed joke about security, and travelers wearing protest buttons found themselves escorted off planes. Passengers often complained about the inconvenience, but neither security guards nor pilots were in the mood to tolerate even a joke about the new risks they faced. In analytic terms, the balance in the system had been recalibrated to prevent more false negatives—allowing people to fly who might later turn out to be a threat—even if that meant far more false positives—subjecting people who were not threats to much greater inconvenience.

On the day before Thanksgiving in November 2002, travelers lined up at New York's La Guardia Airport. Increased security reassured flyers, but air travel remained below the pre–September 11 levels. Transportation Security Administration officials worked to balance the need for additional screening with the job of getting travelers to their planes on time. Several major airlines had temporarily suspended the use of their "self-service" check-ins, forcing all passengers to be processed by airline associates. As seen here, the back-up was often considerable.

In the first years after the September 11 attacks, the new federal Transportation Security Administration (TSA), charged with safeguarding air travel, constantly checked the system's standards. Its officials increased screening for shoes but eased up on files attached to nail clippers. They ratcheted up examination of laptop computers and other electronic equipment but worked to get people through the screening devices more quickly. With the airlines hemorrhaging money and bleeding red on their balance sheets, the TSA wanted to do everything possible to avoid discouraging travel. But everyone knew that nothing could discourage travelers more than another attack. So the TSA worked to identify the most important threats and to focus security screening on them.

The fundamental question became how to find the right balance between allowing false positives and false negatives. At some point, more investment to prevent one kind of error will not prevent the other kind. For example, at some hard-to-define point, a greater investment in passenger screening and luggage searches will not improve airline safety—and it might push potential terrorists to use other techniques instead. Moreover, if policymakers invest more money, energy, expertise, and time in preventing one kind of error, and if they prove successful in preventing attacks, they might conclude that they have invested too much or imposed too much inconvenience. If citizens conclude that they are being overprotected and inconvenienced too greatly, they are likely to press for an easing of restrictions. Money is always tight, and money spent on too much protection could seem wasteful in comparison with other demands on the public treasury, from teachers' salaries to prescription medicines. How can policymakers know how much is enough? Or too much? Even with minimal investment, the country might simply be lucky, as potential terrorists mull over their strategies or shift their tactics. The only way to test how much is enough is to tempt fate by lowering one's guard. Frederickson and LaPorte conclude that "no system is entirely efficient"; therefore, there will always be errors.[5]

This dilemma points to three inescapable tensions in the homeland security system. First, there is the problem of *collecting enough information to make reasoned judgments.* How can policymakers calibrate the system and balance the risks they face? They can use experience and intelligence estimates to frame educated conclusions. The best way to do this is to make a decision, test it to see how well it works, modify it if necessary, and repeat the process. Indeed, many complex, high-risk systems, such as aircraft carriers, provide many opportunities for testing new tactics and gathering feedback. Everything about the process of launching and trapping high-speed jets on a relatively tiny surface bobbing on the waves grows from decades of naval experience.

The fewer opportunities there are to test the system, the harder it is for those who manage it to have confidence they have set just the right balance. That is part of the challenge of running the space shuttle program, which involves only a few launches, each of which carries a high risk. As the investigation into the 2003 disintegration of the shuttle *Columbia* revealed, it had been easy for shuttle managers to talk themselves into the conclusion that their systems were safe, because small mishaps—such as the foam that flew off the external fuel tank and struck the shuttle on launch—had not previously caused major damage. Their confidence proved tragically misplaced. When a large piece of foam flew off the tank and damaged the *Columbia*'s wing, a very rare false negative error proved fatal.[6] Homeland security events can be even rarer. Skillful terrorists constantly seek new cracks in the system. Taken together, these two factors make it extremely difficult—perhaps impossible—for managers to learn how best to set the balance between the two kinds of errors.

The second problem facing homeland security is the *risk of backsliding*. As we saw in previous chapters, powerful forces deeply rooted in the political system can pull against efforts to strengthen homeland security. LaPorte argues that to minimize homeland security risks we will likely be forced to accept more costly false positive errors than we might like, in order to reduce the false negative errors that we cannot accept. We will likely have to accept higher costs and more inconvenience than might be necessary, so as to reduce the risk of terrorist attacks as much as possible. That means that policymakers are likely to be plagued constantly by complaints about overspending, inconvenience, and excessive intrusion into civil rights and civil liberties. As more time goes by without an attack, pressures to reduce false positives are likely to grow, demands to reduce investment in homeland security and shift spending to other areas will increase, and cries to eliminate inconvenience and lessen the invasion of civil rights and civil liberties will ring out louder. Such backsliding might make sense in time, but it could increase the risk of terrorist attacks.

The third issue is the problem of *calibrating risk*. The way people perceive risk is often not in proportion with the objective facts. As Ropeik and Gray found, individuals tend to fear new risks more than existing ones, risks that attract big headlines more than quiet ones, and risks that are controlled by others more than ones they choose.[7] The highly public September 11 attacks, with people watching on live television as one of the planes hit the World Trade Center, terrified many away from flying altogether. As the researchers Slovic and Weber observe, "differences in risk perception lie at the heart of disagreements about the best course of action between technical experts and members of the general public." Indeed, dangers are real, but risks are inherently subjective. Social forces can amplify the sense of danger that individuals feel.[8]

Researchers warn that when feelings are on edge, as in the days after September 11, there is danger that public officials may overreact. So not only is it impossible to know, from analysis, which level of protection is best, but it is just as possible that raw emotions may drive the system to hyperinvestment in some protections that might not, in the long run, really make the country safer. The false-positive costs may rise quickly. That also can encourage backsliding if further attacks do not occur. The homeland security system could thus find itself lurching between extremes of overreacting and underreacting, both of which can make citizens more vulnerable, impose more costs, and further limit personal freedom.

In an effort to address these three concerns, the Pentagon explored an experimental new method to predict what risks were most likely. Its Defense Advanced Research Projects Agency signed a contract with the Policy Analysis Market, an online service, to create a market to allow Middle East experts to bet on likely political and economic events in the region. The Policy Analysis Market would enroll one hundred experts, give each a hypothetical account of $100, and allow them to buy and sell online futures contracts on issues such as the overthrow of one of the region's leaders or whether a major figure such as Yasir Arafat might be assassinated. This was to be a mechanism to collect the judgments of many experts, do it in real time, and allow the assessments to change over time with new events and new analysis. Its value, experts believed, lay in improving the ability of analysts to predict what was likely to happen next. Similar online markets, such as www.tradesports.com, allowed betting on everything from who was going to win the Super Bowl to who was going to win the jackpot on a reality television show. Researchers at the University of Iowa have run a presidential futures market for years, in which anyone can log in, create an account, and bet on who will win the next election.[9]

But the plan died an almost instant death when news stories labeled it state-sponsored "gambling on terrorism," a notion that quickly proved unpalatable to Americans struggling to recover from the deaths of thousands of their fellow citizens. "This is just wrong," said Sen. Tom Daschle, D-S.D. Sen. Byron Dorgan, D-N.D., said it was "unbelievably stupid." Sen. Ron Wyden, D-Ore., observed, "Trading on corn futures is real different than trading on terrorism and atrocity futures. One is morally fine and represents free enterprise, and the other one is morally over the line."[10] The Defense Department analysts believed otherwise. They continued to think that rapidly collecting the best judgment of experts in the field would enhance their assessments of likely threats, but following such a political storm they dared not make their argument publicly.

Analysts have struggled, through both political pressures and great uncertainty, to estimate which problems the nation is likely to face and how best to solve them. Ultimately, the question of how to balance the risks and costs of the homeland security system is one that elected officials must answer. The analysis implicitly warns that people might have to accept higher costs than seem warranted in order to secure the level of protection desired. That will come as little surprise to homeland security experts, but it raises stark warnings for policymakers and citizens alike about the difficulty of balancing risks and costs and of keeping that balance over the long haul.

WARNING SIGNALS

As homeland security officials planned their strategy, they confronted a tough question. Because the intelligence agencies could not connect the dots in advance of the September 11 attacks, the terrorists gained complete surprise. But what if analysts had detected the possibility of an attack in advance? How would the government have notified state and local officials and citizens? How should the government best communicate risk?

In the weeks after the attacks, a flood of new warnings surfaced. Federal officials cautioned that more assaults on planes might occur. They struggled to understand the possibility of more anthrax attacks. Intelligence officials detected "chatter" among suspected terrorists that could be a harbinger of other attacks. In the aftermath of September 11, no federal official wanted the responsibility of knowing—or even suspecting—information about possible attacks without sharing it. State and local officials, however, were already at heightened alert as they tried to guard buildings, roads, bridges, tunnels, airports, power plants, and a host of other possible targets. Vague warnings about the possibility that bad people might at some point do bad things told them nothing about what to do. Some analysts suggested that the constant warnings only increased anxiety without increasing protection, adding that some all-news television channels only aggravated the problem by putting the terror alert level on a constant crawl at the bottom of the screen.

To provide better guidance, Homeland Security Director Tom Ridge, in March 2002, announced a new alert system. The federal government would notify citizens about the level of risk of terrorist attack using five color designations, ranging from green for low risk to red for severe risk. Each level represented a different degree of threat, and each called for different levels of response from citizens and public officials. Ridge started the system with a yellow alert, which indicated an "elevated" level of threat and was supposed to prompt increased surveillance around critical areas and a heightened state of readiness (see Box 5.1).

The new system immediately drew sarcastic jokes from observers and comedians. Writing in the *St. Petersburg Times,* Jan Glidewell said, "It still doesn't tell you what kind of attack is expected or where it is expected, and it doesn't say what you should do while you are on alert. Basically, it seems, your job is to stand or sit in one place, elevate your blood pressure, secrete excess stomach acid and, well, fret, until the color changes and tells you to be more or less agitated."[11] Jay Leno quipped, "This thing is so confusing. Yesterday the alert went from blue to pink; now half the country thinks we're pregnant."[12]

In February 2003, just two weeks into his job as secretary of the new cabinet-level department, Ridge changed the terror warning from yellow to orange because of intelligence that suggested al Qaeda might be preparing for another attack. Intelligence officials worried in particular that terrorists might be plotting biological or chemical attacks, and Ridge suggested that citizens buy plastic sheeting and duct tape to prepare a "safe room." Shoppers, especially in New York and Washington, swamped home supply stores and cleared all the tape and sheeting from the shelves. Some experts, however, doubted that the plastic-and-duct-tape combination would provide much security. Such safe rooms would work only if people put up the protection in advance of an attack, but chemical and biological attacks typically can be detected only after they occur. Moreover, most such chemical and biological agents are harmful only in small areas and sometimes only on contact with the skin. It would make little sense for everyone to lock themselves in on the off chance that an attack might occur. But if an attack

---

Box 5.1 Homeland Security System

---

1. Low Condition (Green). A low risk of terrorist attacks. Federal departments and agencies should develop a process to assure that all facilities and regulated sectors are regularly assessed for vulnerabilities to terrorist attacks and that all reasonable measures are taken to mitigate those vulnerabilities.
2. Guarded Condition (Blue). A general risk of terrorist attacks. Federal departments and agencies should review and update emergency response procedures.
3. Elevated Condition (Yellow). A significant risk of terrorist attacks. Federal departments and agencies should increase surveillance of critical locations; coordinate emergency plans with nearby jurisdictions as appropriate; and implement, as appropriate, contingency and emergency response plans.
4. High Condition (Orange). A high risk of terrorist attacks. Federal departments and agencies should coordinate necessary security efforts with federal, state, and local law enforcement agencies, and the National Guard or other appropriate armed forces organizations; take additional precautions at public events, possibly considering alternative venues or even cancellation; prepare to execute contingency procedures, such as moving to an alternative site or dispersing their workforce; and restrict access to facilities that are threatened to essential personnel only.
5. Severe Condition (Red). A severe risk of terrorist attacks. Not intended to be sustained for substantial periods of time. Federal departments and agencies should increase or redirect personnel to address critical emergency needs; assign emergency response personnel; and pre-position and mobilize specially trained teams or resources; monitor, redirect, or constrain transportation systems; and close public and government facilities.

Source: Adapted from U.S. Department of Homeland Security, "Homeland Security Advisory System" (2004), at www.dhs.gov/dhspublic/display?theme=29.

---

did occur, its effects would arise before anyone could put up the plastic and apply the tape.

Nevertheless, it was hard to argue with Ridge's basic advice. As anyone who has ever attempted a repair knows, duct tape is useful for an infinite variety of problems. Plastic sheets can provide temporary repairs from storm damage or supply temporary shelter if necessary. Together with a battery-operated radio, a flashlight, extra batteries, and a supply of water and food, duct tape and plastic sheeting are useful supplies that can help citizens recover from a wide variety of emergencies, from terrorist attacks to tornadoes. But the commonsense nature of the recommendations became lost in the fuzzy nature of the terrorist warning, and the announcement provided endless material for comedians who could not help themselves.

Online humor columnist Andy Borowitz pointed to Vice President Dick Cheney's connections to private industry to suggest that the vice president had cornered the market on duct tape and plastic sheeting. Ridge's warning, he joked, put untold profits directly into Cheney's pocket. Borowitz then added a suggestion which, he riffed, came from Ridge. "If you see someone you suspect is a terrorist, sneak up behind him and wrap him tightly in duct tape or plastic sheeting." He continued, "This is a simple thing each and every one of us can do." [13] From the late-night television talk shows to *Saturday Night Live* and *The Daily Show*, the jokes came nonstop.

When Ridge was Pennsylvania governor he did not seem quite so funny, wrote *Chicago Sun-Times* columnist William O'Rourke. But with the duct tape episode, Ridge "does his best on his own to make his department look ridiculous." [14] Ridge found himself roasted at the annual Gridiron dinner, at which top journalists and politicians trade off-the-record spoofs. To the tune of the wartime standard "Over There," a journalist playing Ridge and wrapped in duct tape and plastic sheeting, sang, "We're sealed, we're shipshape / The axis of evil lives in fear / Over here, over here." [15] The wife of Bush budget director Mitchell E. Daniels Jr. said that the message for the upcoming Valentine's Day holiday should be "Say it with duct tape." Daniels obliged and asked the florist to send his wife a special bouquet with the stems wrapped in the tape. "I think they got into it," Daniels said of the florist. [16]

But beyond the jokes, many observers worried that the duct tape episode showed real problems in the nation's homeland security strategy. A columnist for London's *Guardian* wrote that it had taught him "that the country's rulers haven't the faintest idea what they are doing." [17] Former Democratic presidential candidate Gary Hart put the point more sharply: "Because the government has done so little against terrorism at home, it sounded as if they were saying, 'You're on your own.'" Homeland security expert Ivo H. Daalder added, "Homeland security is a difficult job, but they've been at it for 17 months, and they're certainly not getting any better at it.... They want to be absolutely sure that if anything happens they can say they've warned us about it. But by covering their backsides, they're making terrorism into something more awful." [18]

Ridge and his staff faced a tough, perhaps impossible challenge. No one wanted casualties to occur because the public did not have access to all the information available. On the other hand, because terrorists are secretive and unpredictable, the best that the Department of Homeland Security could typically do was to share a sense that risks had increased, that something might happen somewhere. Department officials could never say that a particular thing would happen at a particular place at a particular time. Indeed, if the department had such specific information it surely would work with law enforcement officials to arrest the

perpetrators. The nature of the risk was always vague. Sometimes intelligence officials detected more specific threats, such as a plot to attack New York's Brooklyn
Bridge, but the intelligence supporting the threat was often not solid enough to
broadcast the specifics publicly. Often the best that government officials could do
was to suggest that people—and local officials—needed to be even more careful
than usual. But vague warnings, some suggested, only increased fear without increasing security.

A 2003 study by the Congressional Research Service (CRS) concluded that the
color-coded alert system was too vague. In the system's first eighteen months, the
Department of Homeland Security had raised the terror alert to orange four
times, but the nonspecific explanations of the changes left many analysts fearing
that the department would lose credibility. People might simply begin taking
them less seriously and undermine the department's efforts. The DHS-issued
warnings included few specifics about what citizens and government officials were
supposed to do except to be more careful. Moreover, state and local officials complained that they often did not receive news about the changed alert level from the
DHS and had to rely on the news media. The chief of the Portland, Maine, police
department said he relied on CNN. On one occasion when the threat level was
raised, the official notification came eight hours after he saw it on the news channel. When warnings occurred, responding to them was expensive for local officials, who sometimes resisted. Philadelphia mayor John F. Street, for example,
refused to close a street near Independence Hall following a DHS warning.
Moreover, CRS found, the DHS system was one of eight separate warning systems about potential catastrophes—severe weather, contamination from chemical
and biological weapons stockpiles, and presidential alerts, among others—which
were not integrated.[19]

The United Kingdom, which has long struggled with terrorist attacks by the
Irish Republican Army, uses a different system. Home Secretary David Blunkett,
whose department is in charge of UK's homeland security, explained it this way:

> We have internally seven different layers of threat level. We announce the
> heightened threat level only when we believe that the public themselves are at
> risk, or when we have to take obvious action, as we did six weeks ago [in early
> 2003] to ensure that there wasn't a threat to Heathrow Airport. In other words,
> we're pronouncing publicly at a moment when we believe either that we should
> engage the public in their own surveillance, or at a moment when the threat
> level has heightened to a position where either in heightened policing or in
> terms of using military hardware, as we did six weeks ago, it would be obvious
> to the public that we're taking action.[20]

The British policy tipped the balance of public access versus secrecy of sources
toward secrecy. The Web site of the British Home Office told citizens, "We are
committed to giving you as much information as we can about terrorism." But, it
added, "we also have a responsibility to protect people working in the intelligence

and security fields," and the government wanted to avoid giving out "information that could compromise their safety."[21]

British officials resisted the American color-coded system as far too broad and vague. As the Home Office explained,

> We do not believe it is beneficial to the UK to have one single national system to indicate the current general level of threat. Rather than one blanket system, we operate specific systems in various public sectors and key industries, like aviation and the utilities. This reflects the fact that when alert states need to be raised in one sector, the threat assessment for other sectors could stay the same. Our concern is always to minimise the damage to the economy and our prosperity caused by alarms of this nature.[22]

As the nation moved deeper into the new post–September 11 era, government officials worked on fine-tuning the alert system. Over the 2003 Christmas and New Year's Eve holidays, the federal government intercepted terrorist chatter that suggested the possibility of imminent attacks on a scale that might exceed those of September 11. Ridge raised the nation's alert status from yellow to orange, and then, after the holidays passed uneventfully, he lowered the alert level back to yellow. These changes fueled the campaign of Rep. Jim Turner, D-Texas, for revisions in the alert system. He believed that nationwide alerts unnecessarily alarmed citizens, wasted resources where threats were lower, and failed to focus sufficient attention where threats were higher. David Heyman at the Center for Strategic and International Studies estimated that raising the alert level costs federal, state, and local officials, as well as private companies, more than $1 billion a week in additional security costs. Ridge acknowledged that regional alerts might be possible, and he warned that some airports and sites around the country would remain at a higher state of alert. "We will maintain particular vigilance around some critical resources and locales," he said in January 2004, but he refused to say which sites would remain at the higher alert level.[23] The episode demonstrated the government's search for making the alerts more precise while minimizing the risk that security might remain too low in some areas.

The British also worked on devising better technical systems for alerting citizens in case of danger. In New York, the September 11 terrorist attack not only destroyed the two World Trade Center towers, but they also took out a major telephone switching center, many cellular phone towers, and the transmitters of a number of New York television stations, which had sat atop one of the towers. In Manchester, Leeds, and Liverpool, British officials had already installed a pager warning system. After September 11, the British Home Office further evaluated using new technologies, including pagers, instant messaging, e-mail, and digital services to transmit warnings. When the September 11 attacks overwhelmed cellular phone service in Washington, but left Blackberry wireless e-mail service relatively unaffected, congressional leaders issued each member of Congress a Blackberry to transmit emergency evacuation messages and keep the members in touch in case of another attack.

Of course, other problems also proved capable of seriously disrupting communications. The massive August 2003 blackout that darkened vast portions of the Midwest and Northeast in the United States as well as parts of Canada swamped and then cut off cellular telephone service in some cities, in particular New York. Without electric power, citizens could not turn on their televisions to receive timely updates. Many relied on battery-operated radios and word of mouth to learn, to their relief, that the blackout was just a blackout, not a terrorist attack.

Public officials needed to determine how best to educate citizens about the new risks they faced without "crying wolf" or aggravating an already scary situation. They needed to couple warnings with specific responses or risk losing credibility. They needed to get the word out, quickly and effectively, to the frontline first responders who would have to deal with any attack that occurred, along with specific advice about what to do, when, and where. And they needed to develop the technical means of communicating advice in ways that would get through in case of an emergency that disrupted communication systems.

TRUST

Despite the warnings, jokes, and debates about technology, these issues fundamentally boil down to politics and values. The greatest difficulties of coordinating homeland security are not the managerial ones. Post–September 11 public opinion polls showed that many Americans wanted government to play a stronger role in protecting them from future attacks.[24] What kind of government role citizens wanted, however, varied significantly. In a poll taken a year after the attacks, Americans favored creation of a national identification card by a two-to-one majority. Support for monitoring of cell phone calls, however, had dropped from 54 percent to 32 percent.[25] Citizens wanted safety, but they were unsure about what that meant or what price they ought to pay.

Two fundamental problems characterize the task of framing homeland security policy. One is the level of security that public officials can responsibly guarantee. Citizens, not surprisingly, expect full protection from all risks. They look to their government to provide it, and they criticize public agencies and officials when problems occur. The revelations that FBI field agents in Minneapolis and Phoenix had identified suspicious individuals receiving flight training in advance of September 11 led to widespread criticism of the intelligence agencies and, ultimately, to the creation of the Department of Homeland Security. Government officials plan and train, budget and design, coordinate and test, but they can never cover all contingencies. They can never fully *guarantee* protection to citizens—they can only guarantee their best efforts. On the other hand, an argument that officials did their very best could prove a thin reed on which to rest the full defense of their work.

The other problem is that security cannot be pursued in isolation. Rather, it is the product of continual trade-offs between protection from risks and limits on freedom. Just how far are citizens willing to go to secure protection? Which freedoms are they willing to sacrifice, and to what degree? Are they willing to accept the implicit risk that comes when citizens rise up to defend their freedoms? Are their tolerances of risks and of limits on freedom likely to change as September 11 recedes into the past?

In the American intergovernmental system we tolerate constant battles over boundaries, responsibilities, and accountability, in part because we appreciate being able to take our complaints to multiple venues and in part because we cherish local self-government, even if it is inefficient. Homeland security, however, puts tough new demands on the intergovernmental system. For the homeland truly to be secure, federalism will need to accommodate a tightly knit administrative structure that produces high levels of reliable services.

The civil rights battles in the last half of the twentieth century focused the debate over how much discretion state and local governments ought to have at the expense of nationally guaranteed rights. Homeland security produces the same tension between national power and local discretion but does so in a context that, in an instant, could prove fatally unforgiving. National defense is mainly a function of the national government, although the National Guard, managed by the states, plays a role. Homeland security is inevitably an intergovernmental function, with the national government using intelligence to identify security risks and state and local governments fielding the forces that provide security and manage the consequences of any attack. Homeland security therefore challenges governmental leaders to balance the political attributes of federalism with the imperative of forging state and local governments into a reliable system that, in fact, makes the homeland safer.

Homeland security is thus far more than a technical issue. It is more than a national security issue or a puzzle of federalism. It is, at its core, a problem of governance. And it is one that demands strong and effective political leadership to make the necessary decisions and to shape the necessary trade-offs.

Public officials and citizens rarely discuss these big political trade-offs explicitly. Amid tough and sometimes insoluble problems, it is easier to build consensus and cobble together coalitions if some of the toughest issues are kept vague and the most difficult trade-offs are pushed to the background. That helps make politics work. Making everything explicit can make the trade-offs—who wins and especially who loses—all too painfully clear. Politics runs on the subtext; new battles are the product of past victories and losses. Any deficit from one battle can potentially be made up in the next. Terrorism, however, has made that game much harder to play. The enormous losses of September 11 were vivid and painful, and the implications of further attacks were clear. A political system traditionally built on keeping such trade-offs below the surface suddenly has found itself grappling with them in the open.

This is a key challenge that can only be solved through political leadership. The job of leaders is to define reality for others.[26] They help resolve ambiguity. They motivate employees and they are the faces an organization presents to the world. They build and maintain administrative capacity. Most importantly, they fill the gaps that other processes and strategies leave. They are responsible for effective operation across government's complex boundaries and problems. In homeland security, that means defining what level of risk is acceptable, and how to set the balance between freedom and security that any level of risk entails.

Leaders must shoulder the burden of defining, and accepting accountability for, decisions that have profound implications, stretching to the very safety and survival of citizens. That is a huge responsibility with equally huge political implications. It requires public officials to gently feel their way toward defining acceptable levels of risk and appropriate ways of holding officials accountable for securing them. It requires them to make critical decisions about the balance of risk and protection, something in which they did not have much experience before September 11. As Richard A. Clarke, former White House counterterrorism coordinator, said, "Democracies don't prepare well for things that have never happened before."[27]

At the core of these difficult challenges for democracy is the role of citizens. For all the jokes about duct tape and plastic sheets, the issue revolved around the responsibility that citizens can—and should—play in homeland security. How much information should citizens receive? What should they do with it? Which risks are acceptable—and what price should be paid for reducing them? How much protection is possible—and reasonable—in the risky and uncertain world of homeland security? To what degree should citizens hold public officials accountable for these decisions? Few issues of democracy and political leadership have been so difficult. Faced with such tough puzzles, it became tempting for leaders and citizens alike to try to duck the trade-offs and slide back to the more comfortable—if far more risky—world they had known before September 11.

Chapter

6

Civil Rights and
Civil Liberties

OF ALL THE SURPRISES IN THE AFTERMATH of the September 11 terrorist attacks, one of the biggest was the discovery that the four teams of hijackers had been living undetected in the United States for many months. Two had settled in San Diego in January 2000. Several had spent time in the United States in the early 1990s, taking language instruction and, later, flight lessons. The "muscle" hijackers, whose job it was to overcome the pilots and control the passengers, began arriving in April 2001. The four pilot hijackers flew dry runs across the country early in the year and, for reasons investigators could never determine, spent layovers in Las Vegas.[1]

All of the hijackers had entered the country with what appeared to be valid passports. By the day of the attacks, the visas of two of them had expired, and a third hijacker had failed to register for classes and thus violated the terms of his student visa. But federal authorities did not discover any of this until after the attacks. Just as importantly, sixteen of the hijackers were in the country legally. All managed to live comfortable lives, blending into the fabric of American society.

Americans have always treasured their ability to go where they want when they want. They have long valued the freedom to choose their jobs and chart their careers, to live their lives without government scrutiny, and to associate with people of their own choosing. So important are these values, in fact, that many states refused to ratify the U.S. Constitution until, in 1789, Congress proposed a bill of rights. But at the same time, Americans have always expected their government to protect them from threats. That the country was attacked by people who had so easily integrated themselves into the nation's daily life raised a dilemma: How much should government intrude into the lives of citizens in its quest to provide protection?

That question raised a second point. Americans have always accepted any expansion of government power grudgingly. When government has expanded, people have tended to trust state and local governments, to which they are closer, more than the federal government. But to the degree that homeland security strengthens government power, it tends to strengthen the power of the federal government. Therefore, it not only shifts the balance from individual freedom to government control, but it also shifts the balance from state and local authority to federal power. In the long run, the most lasting and important effects of the September 11 attacks could prove to be these changes in individual liberty and governance.

The discovery that the attackers had so easily entered the country and managed to plot the attacks without detection (except by a handful of suspicious FBI agents, whose memos had not gained attention at headquarters) stunned federal officials. A congressional investigation, completed in 2002 but whose report was not released until six months later in early 2003, offered a scathing assessment. "At home, the counterterrorism effort suffered from the lack of an effective domestic intelligence capability. The FBI was unable to identify and monitor effectively the extent of activity by al Qaeda and other international terrorist groups operating in the United States." Coupled with the CIA's problems in tracking foreign threats, "these problems greatly exacerbated the nation's vulnerability to an increasingly dangerous and immediate international terrorist threat inside the United States."[2] Sixteen of the nineteen hijackers had come from Saudi Arabia, and an American who had worked for the Saudi foreign ministry said, "The visa operation is a joke over there." Nationals from other countries handled the initial processing of the applications, and that made it easy for even questionable individuals to slip through the process. "The State Department does not do a quality control check," the former employee charged. As a result, *Boston Globe* reporters concluded, "With its borders so porous and its recordkeeping so unreliable, the United States has little ability to keep all criminals—or terrorists—out of the country and has no system to track them once they're in."[3]

According to the *Washington Post*, the whole star-crossed system was "a portrait of terrorists who took advantage of America's open society as they planned their murderous assault on the Pentagon and the World Trade Center."[4] The story was dismaying: a student visa process that one terrorist had exploited; easy issuance of new passports to foreign travelers; a lack of careful screening at American immigration facilities; failure to create effective watch lists and match them to those trying to enter the country; and weak information systems to track foreign travelers once they entered the country. Americans and their officials wondered if the nation's tradition of openness and minimal intrusion of government had allowed the hijackers an advantage that they had exploited to horrendous result.

Americans were rocked not only by the enormity of the attacks but also by the fact that the terrorists had walked among them for months or years. Even worse, intelligence analysts warned that more al Qaeda operatives might be waiting in "sleeper cells" to stage more attacks. Investigators found evidence that some of the September 11 hijackers had studied crop dusters. Was al Qaeda planning to distribute anthrax or some other biotoxin from the air? Was another round of air-line hijackings in the offing? How could the nation protect itself without turning into a police state? The *Boston Globe* said that the terrorists "exploited one of the most enduring tenets of American freedom: its open society."[5] A week after the attacks, columnist Martin Wolf sharply summarized the budding dilemma in London's *Financial Times*. "The biggest long-term challenge to any open society vulnerable to assaults on so vast a scale is striking the balance between safety and freedom. The attack of September 11 took advantage of the ease of movement and low security levels of air transport inside the U.S." He concluded, "We must balance the needs of security with the demands of freedom."[6]

Even the staunchest advocates of civil liberties knew that the horror of the September 11 attacks and the fact that the terrorists had exploited American free-dom in an effort to weaken the nation would inevitably mean some sacrifice of civil rights and civil liberties to provide greater security. Intelligence analysts dis-covered that the terrorists were using satellite phones and coded e-mail. By con-trast, American officials charged with guarding the borders and ferreting out terrorist cells had to sift through reams of paper and deal with databases that did not connect and computer systems that could not network. Sen. Edward M. Kennedy of Massachusetts, long an advocate of an open immigration policy, nonetheless recognized that things had to change. "We're dealing with horse-and-buggy technology," he said. "We're dealing with handwritten notes. It's a shock-ing indictment."[7] U.S. intelligence had to enter the twenty-first century.

PASSING THE PATRIOT ACT

For the Justice Department officials shaping the new policy, the issue also had a sharp personal side. Barbara Olson, a CNN commentator and the wife of Solici-tor General Ted Olson, had been aboard American Airlines flight 77. Olson called her husband from the plane twice to ask him what she and her fellow pas-sengers ought to do. Soon it did not matter—flight 77 crashed into the Pentagon, killing everyone on board. The officials working on the new policy had known Barbara Olson well. Her story gave them an extra measure of determination. Ter-rorism had taken on a personal face.

Attorney General John Ashcroft, along with other senior administration offi-cials, was at a secure location, a carefully guarded and undisclosed site away from Washington, for the first days after the attacks. But Ashcroft sent word to his staff that he wanted tough, new authority to help the FBI and the Justice Department find and break up terrorist cells. One of his aides later remembered that Ashcroft's charge was clear: "all that is necessary for law enforcement, within the bounds of the Constitution, to discharge the obligation to fight this war against terror."[8] Not only did department officials feel the need to act, but the heat of press scrutiny created an inescapable need to be *seen* to be acting as well.

That imperative created a flurry of proposals on the floor of Congress. Some members proposed an aggressive new authority that would allow the federal government to intercept e-mail and telephone calls. Proposals surfaced to allow the government to increase monitoring of foreign agents and to infiltrate religious services even if there was no prior evidence of criminal activity. Investigators, in fact, had complained that the law made it easier to infiltrate the Mafia than al Qaeda cells and this had to be corrected. For their part, civil libertarians worried that Congress would rush to enact sweeping new legislation without stopping to consider what impact it might have on civil rights and civil liberties. Security experts struggled to find a way to balance concerns for liberty with the need for stronger homeland defense.

A plan began to take shape. Members of Congress agreed on new legislation to make it easier to track the origin and destination of telephone calls and to increase the authority of government to track e-mail. They agreed on broader wiretap authority and new measures to track the flow of money to terrorist groups. The Bush administration, however, wanted to go much further. Ashcroft, for example, wanted the authority to indefinitely detain noncitizens who the Justice Department believed might be planning acts of terrorism. He wanted greater flexibility in sharing grand jury and eavesdropping data throughout the federal government and in tapping into e-mail chats. And he wanted the new authority to be made permanent, so that the federal government could create new and aggressive long-term strategies to go after potential terrorists. Just a week after the attacks, Ashcroft announced at a press conference that he expected the administration's proposal to be ready very shortly—and that he wanted Congress to act on it within a few days. "We need these tools to fight the terrorism threat which exists in the United States," Ashcroft said.[9]

Most members of Congress agreed that the nation needed tougher penalties for terrorists and that the federal government needed broader investigative powers. But Sen. Patrick J. Leahy, D-Vt., chair of the Judiciary Committee, warned that "the biggest mistake we could make" was to conclude that the terrorist threat was so great "that we don't need the Constitution."[10] He added, "The first thing we have to realize is this is not either/or—this is not the Constitution versus capturing the terrorists. We can have both."[11] The American Civil Liberties Union echoed Leahy's concern in a set of ten principles endorsed by scores of civil rights and civil liberties groups. "We need to consider proposals calmly and deliberately with a determination not to erode the liberties and freedoms that are at the core of the American way of life," the ACLU said on September 20.[12]

Fundamental issues were at stake. Citizens expect a right of privacy in their homes and workplaces, but government intelligence analysts believed that they needed broader powers to wiretap phones and track e-mail. They sought new powers to search the homes and belongings of individuals suspected to have terrorist links, without informing the individuals in advance. The rationale behind all of this was that the government suspected that terrorists worked in secret cells. Conducting a search of one cell member's home might alert the others that the government was on to them and frustrate the government's ability to arrest all of the cell's members.

Civil libertarians worried that in its zeal to capture and interrogate potential terrorists, the government might violate the long-standing principle of habeas corpus. Literally translated as "you have the body," the principle traces its lineage back to the Magna Carta. A writ of habeas corpus, issued by a court, requires the government to bring a prisoner to court to show that it has reasonable cause for holding the person or the prisoner must be released. Federal officials said they believed that some potential terrorists should be held as "enemy combatants," which would allow them to be imprisoned indefinitely, without trial, to permit prolonged investigation and questioning. That, civil libertarians worried, would open the door to broad abuse of government power.

Congress did not come close to meeting Ashcroft's deadline, but it did complete its work in near-record time. The legislation's authors formally labeled it the "Uniting and Strengthening America by Providing Appropriate Tools Required to Intercept and Obstruct Terrorism Act"—or the "USA Patriot Act," surely one of the most clever and symbolically powerful Washington acronyms of all time. It not only found the right words to spell out the title for the act, but it wrapped the legislation in the cloak of patriotism, which the drafters hoped no one could resist in the frightening days after September 11. The bill won House approval on October 24. The Senate agreed the next day by a vote of 98–1, with Sen. Russ Feingold, D-Wis., casting the only "nay" vote. President Bush signed the bill promptly on October 26, just six weeks after the attacks. "Today, we take an essential step in defeating terrorism, while protecting the constitutional rights of all Americans," Bush said that morning. "With my signature, this law will give intelligence and law enforcement officials important new tools to fight a present danger."[13]

The USA Patriot Act gives the federal government broad new powers to investigate and detain potential terrorists:[14]

- It facilitates the tracking and gathering of information with new technologies. The law allows federal officials greater authority to use a kind of "secret caller ID," which can identify the source and destination of calls made to and from a particular telephone. Existing laws allowed such "trap and trace" orders for phone calls. The new law permits them for other electronic communications, including e-mail.
- The law permits "roving surveillance," which means that surveillance can occur without being limited to a particular place or instrument. In the past, court orders allowed surveillance only on telephones or places identified in advance. Since terrorists often change locations and sometimes discard cellular tele-

phones after a single use, court orders could not keep up with their activities. The new law permits investigators to obtain authority to track targets as they move or switch phones and e-mails. It also allows investigators to obtain a court order to examine any "tangible item," rather than just business records. For example, investigators can probe voice mails and library records showing who borrowed which books.

- It increases federal authority to investigate money laundering. The new law requires financial institutions to keep more complete records of the financial activities of suspicious individuals and to allow federal investigators broader access to them. In the aftermath of September 11, federal officials had discovered that hundreds of thousands of dollars had flowed through the financial system to terrorist cells undetected, and they wanted stronger authority to trace this flow of money.

- The law strengthens the authority of border agents to prevent possible terrorists from entering the United States. It gives authorities greater power to detain and deport suspicious individuals and those suspected of supporting them. To signal that these provisions were not aimed at punishing foreigners, the law also provides humanitarian assistance for foreign victims of the September 11 attacks.

- The law defines a broad array of activities—terrorist attacks on mass transportation facilities, biological attacks, harboring of terrorists, money laundering to support terrorism, and fraudulent solicitation of money to support terrorism— as federal crimes. Federal officials were concerned that the ingenuity of terrorists had grown faster than criminal law, and they were intent on capturing the full range of terrorist activities as crimes.

- It allows so-called sneak-and-peek searches in which investigators can enter homes and facilities and conduct searches without informing those searched until sometime later. Under previous law, those searched had to be informed before the search began. Federal officials said that giving even a few minutes' notice might disrupt their investigations and tip off members of a terrorist cell. Sneak-and-peek searches, they said, permit more effective investigations.

- It expands the government's authority to prosecute computer hackers. Government officials increasingly worried that terrorists, or even ordinary hackers, would exploit vulnerabilities in the Internet to flood the system with e-mail or to damage computer records. With the growing dependence of the world economy on electronic commerce and communication, officials wanted to increase the system's protection against cyber-terror attacks and to provide stronger remedies to those hurt by hackers. Such attacks had not occurred on a broad scale at that point, but security analysts warned that the system was vulnerable and that they could occur in the future. Over the next few years, hackers proved them right.

Administration officials maintained that the USA Patriot Act gave the government valuable new powers that only terrorists needed to fear. The line, often repeated, was that the government needed the same power to investigate potential terrorists that it had long used to stop organized crime. Civil rights experts acknowledged the need for new government powers but worried that there were few checks on the new powers and that the government would push them too far. The government could conduct searches without informing those searched. It could hold prisoners without informing them of the charges or bringing them to trial. And the issue not only was *what* the government could do. It was also the uncertainty about how the new powers would be used and what protections citizens would have to ensure that government officials did not abuse those powers.

For the new wiretap and surveillance powers, the law created a "sunset" (an automatic expiration of the authority) at the end of 2005, unless Congress extended them. Within an hour of Bush's signing the act, Ashcroft put ninety-four federal attorneys and fifty-six FBI field offices to work implementing its provisions. In September 2003, he hailed the Patriot Act as one of the Justice Department's best tools to "connect the dots" in fighting terrorist activity.[15] Congress passed the law with overwhelming, bipartisan support. But almost immediately, critics began worrying about just how the government would use the act's new powers.

BROADENING THE WAR

In his September 20, 2001, address to a joint session of Congress, President Bush condemned the Taliban government in Afghanistan for sheltering al Qaeda terrorists. He bluntly demanded, "Deliver to United States authorities all the leaders of al Qaeda who hide in your land." Bush continued, "These demands are not open to negotiation or discussion. The Taliban must act, and act immediately. They will hand over the terrorists, or they will share in their fate."[16] A few weeks later, Bush made good on his threat, launching a major military campaign in Afghanistan, and in less than a week, the United States and its allies swept the Taliban forces from most of the northern part of the country.

The October 2001 military campaign quickly brought into the spotlight the issue of the rights that should be accorded suspected terrorists. As U.S. forces captured territory in Afghanistan, they also captured members of al Qaeda, along with other suspected enemy combatants and Taliban soldiers. How should the United States treat non-Americans that officials suspected were terrorists? What about armed fighters allied with governments, such as the Taliban, that had sheltered terrorists? What rights should those captured be granted, and how, if at all, should those rights differ from those guaranteed Americans? President Bush had promised that the war on terrorism would be a new kind of war. The new kind of war also raised new issues for how to treat those involved in it, as well as those associated with the war on the United States.

These big questions broke out into still others: What about issues of security? Captured terrorists had to be held securely so that they could not escape or be freed by their colleagues. U.S. officials also wanted to minimize the chance of hostage taking, with the terrorists' colleagues trying to bargain for their release. Who would have authority to try the terrorists, and where would such trials take place? How could the United States pursue trials without undermining the intelligence value of captured al Qaeda members? Indeed, did those involved in terrorism deserve trials? If so, how long could they be held before the trials occurred? What punishments could be meted out? Given the widespread opposition to the death penalty in many parts of the world, especially among European allies of the United States, would executing suspected terrorists be considered?

The United States decided to place captured individuals under tight guard at the American naval base at Guantanamo, Cuba. The base, the nation's oldest beyond its shores and the only one in a communist country, dates from a 1903 lease to establish a coaling station for naval vessels. For the military's purposes, it was a great choice: far from the Middle East and South Asia, surrounded by water and communist Cuba, the compound was easy to control and difficult to penetrate. It was on American-controlled soil but outside the United States, so officials could assert that different rights and liberties applied to prisoners held there. In January 2002, the government established "Camp X-Ray," a bare-bones installation to house the first of the captured fighters and suspected terrorists. International criticism immediately erupted. When the first prisoners were flown to Guantanamo from Afghanistan, they were blindfolded and kept in heavy restraints and earmuffs. Their beards had been shaved—an action considered by many to be a sacrilegious insult to the prisoners' Islamic faith. Pictures of those held outraged human rights activists, especially in Europe. Other photographs showed prisoners kneeling shackled in front of wire cages with corrugated metal roofs, which served as temporary cells. Critics charged that the prisoners were being held unlawfully, without a right to trial and other rights customary under international law, and that they were being treated inhumanely, deprived of adequate shelter and the practice of their religion.

At first, senior American officials maintained that the Guantanamo prisoners were not prisoners of war but "unlawful combatants," armed fighters who are not covered by the portions of the Geneva Conventions that guarantee humane treatment for anyone captured in combat. According to the Geneva Conventions, prisoners of war have certain guaranteed rights and need only give interrogators their name, rank, and serial number. While many foreign government officials and human rights advocates did acknowledge that the prisoners were not clearly entitled to prisoner-of-war status because they did not wear uniforms, fight for a regular army, or respect the rules of war, images in the media suggested to many critics that those guarantees were not being met. Human Rights Watch, a monitoring group, charged that the United States had implicitly acknowledged that the conditions were inadequate when officials stated that more permanent facilities would soon be constructed. Indeed, the military began construction of

"Camp Delta" shortly thereafter. The facility opened in 2003 and was equipped to house more than eight hundred detainees.

As their detention stretched on, however, new problems surfaced. In the first fourteen months, at least fourteen prisoners attempted suicide. Outside experts said that the prisoners faced enormous stress, in part because of their isolation (they were kept apart except for two fifteen-minute exercise periods each day) and uncertainty (since they were far from home and did not know when their detention would end). Prisoners who cooperated, both by observing the rules and providing useful information, could win transfer to better, barracks-style quarters, where they were less isolated. That option, however, scarcely satisfied the critics. Human Rights Watch charged, "Rather than relying on international law as an essential tool in the fight against terrorism, the Bush Administration increasingly treated it as an encumbrance. An increasingly powerful faction within the Bush Administration pursued a radical vision of the United States as above international law."[17] Administration officials rejected the charge, saying that the detainees were being treated humanely, and they reminded critics that the nation had a responsibility to learn as much as possible from the prisoners to reduce the threat of future attacks.

Most difficult were the matters of how long the prisoners would be held and what kind of court would deal with them. Critics both in the United States and abroad argued that the administration could not simply hold the prisoners indefinitely, without charging them with a crime or trying them. Over the first two years the number of prisoners grew, and only a handful were released. American officials decided that any trials would not be held in American courts but in military tribunals, which would have the power to impose the death penalty on those found guilty of capital offenses. The detainees included citizens not only of Middle Eastern and South Asian countries but also of European nations such as the United Kingdom, which prohibited capital punishment. The prospect of U.S. action that violated the laws and policies of other nations severely strained international relations. Tensions with other nations and with human rights groups grew when the government disclosed that the military was holding children among the Guantanamo detainees.

The constraints that foreign and domestic concern about human rights imposed on its actions led the government to keep the highest-ranking terrorist officials in high-security sites in Afghanistan or to surreptitiously ship them to foreign intelligence services less restrained in their interrogation practices. In Afghanistan, for example, metal shipping containers behind three layers of concertina wire held top al Qaeda and Taliban officials. Detainees who refused to cooperate could find themselves kept blindfolded and standing or kneeling for hours. In addition, their captors might deprive them of sleep with constant bright lights—called the "stress and duress" technique. Those who cooperated, on the other hand, received creature comforts.

At a news conference in southern Spain in December 2003, Sodia Ali Hossain Kahalon held up the photo of her son, Hamed Abderrahman Ahmed, whom American officials were holding at the special detention facility for suspected terrorists in Guantanamo Bay, Cuba. Spain was a vocal supporter of America's anti-terrorism campaign, but the arrest touched off strong complaints by Spanish government officials. Foreign Minister Ana Palacio said that the United States had made a "major error" in detaining prisoners indefinitely, without being charged or brought to trial, and she warned that "this situation cannot continue."

Interrogators used other techniques to keep captives off balance. For example, they might use disguises and decor to make detainees think they were in another country, perhaps one noted for brutal treatment. They might have female intelligence officers conduct the questioning, which has often proved shocking to prisoners from the male-dominated Muslim culture. The CIA does not always conduct such interrogations; sometimes CIA officials rely on foreign agents under

CIA direction. All of these techniques pressed the boundaries of acceptable techniques and, as one official who supervised the process frankly said, "If you don't violate someone's human rights some of the time, you probably aren't doing your job." [18]

Sometimes the United States relied on what it termed "operational flexibility" to transfer especially difficult and important prisoners to third-party countries, especially Jordan, Egypt, and Morocco. According to one American official involved in this process—known as "extraordinary renditions"—the United States handed over such prisoners along with a list of questions it wanted answered. The understanding was, "We don't kick the [expletive] out of them. We send them to other countries so *they* can kick the [expletive] out of them." Others involved in these activities noted that some countries have used so-called truth serums, such as sodium pentathol, in the questioning. The official American position was, "We're not aware of any torture or even physical abuse." But there was little doubt that, at the very least, these prisoners suffered considerable unpleasantness. At most, they might have suffered physical abuse at the hands of interrogators working closely with the CIA. [19]

THE BUILDING STORM

In the months after the passage of the USA Patriot Act, worries about the ramifications of post–September 11 policies on civil rights and civil liberties steadily grew. Constant criticism from international human rights organizations of U.S. treatment of Taliban and al Qaeda prisoners failed to attract much attention within the United States. At least initially, many Americans were simply in no mood to worry about the possible mistreatment of those allied with the September 11 terrorists. For the USA Patriot Act, however, domestic criticism was broad based and sharp. The legislatures of Alaska and Hawaii passed resolutions condemning it. So did the councils of more than 160 local governments, including Baltimore, Denver, Detroit, Minneapolis, Oakland, San Francisco, and Seattle. Alaska Rep. Don Young, a Republican, said, "I think the Patriot Act was not really thought out." He added, "I'm very concerned that, in our desire for security and our enthusiasm for pursuing supposed terrorists, sometimes we might be on the verge of giving up the freedoms which we're trying to protect." [20] Attorney General Ashcroft decided to meet the critics head-on by going on an eighteen-city speaking tour in August 2003 to sell the act and its accomplishments. It was an unusual tactic by such a senior official for a program that had been in place so long.

Critics on both the right and the left complained that Congress had rushed to judgment. They charged that, under heavy pressure to act, Congress had given too little attention to the measure's effects on civil rights and civil liberties. At the conservative Cato Institute, Robert A. Levy said that "Congress's rush job" had produced a bill that was "unconstitutionally vague" and dangerous. In fact, he charged, the bill gutted "much of the Fourth Amendment [the protection against unreasonable searches and seizures] in far less time than Congress typically expends on routine bills that raise no constitutional concerns." The Patriot Act, Levy said, did not provide sufficient judicial oversight to prevent possible abuses. He contended that the law was too broad and that it aggressively threatened the rights of individual citizens under the guise of protecting against terrorism. He worried that the sunset was too narrow and too long—that the law did not provide a sufficient opportunity to revisit the broad questions to see how well it was working. "Any attempt by government to chip away at constitutionally guaranteed rights must be subjected to the most painstaking scrutiny to determine whether less invasive means could accomplish the same ends. The USA-Patriot anti-terrorism bill does not survive that demanding test. In a free society, we deserve better," he concluded.[21]

From the left came equally harsh criticism. "In its rush to pass the Patriot Act just six weeks after the September 11 attacks, Congress overlooked one of our most fundamental rights—the right to express our political beliefs, especially those that are controversial," said senior attorney Nancy Chang of the Center for Constitutional Rights, which filed suit to block the act. Chang added, "Now it is up to the judiciary to correct Congress's excesses."[22] The ACLU filed its own suit against the Patriot Act, claiming that the provision allowing broader searches of "tangible things" was unconstitutional. Even librarians found themselves in the battle. They feared that the extensive powers the act gave the government to probe "tangible things" would enable federal investigators to examine the reading habits of their patrons without their knowledge or consent. These actions, the American Library Association (ALA) warned in a 2003 resolution, could "threaten civil rights and liberties guaranteed under the United States Constitution and Bill of Rights."[23] That drew a retaliatory charge from Ashcroft, in the midst of his multicity campaign, that the ALA was fueling a "baseless hysteria."[24]

The charges and countercharges finally led the Justice Department to release a count of how many times the "tangible thing" provision had been used in the act's first two years: zero. Department officials argued that this was evidence that the critics did not need to worry. The critics countered that if the provision had not been used at all, it could not have been important in the antiterror war. Rep. John Conyers Jr., D-Mich., said that "if this authority was not needed to investigate September 11," he wondered if "it should stay on the books any longer."[25]

Other worries about the act led C. L. Otter, a Republican member of Congress from Idaho, to champion an amendment to eliminate funding for the Justice Department's sneak-and-peek searches. Otter stunned the administration by winning House passage of the amendment by an overwhelming vote of 309–118. The Justice Department counterattacked by labeling it the "Terrorist Tip-Off Amendment" and said that if terrorists and their colleagues had advance warning of searches they could quickly break up their cells and reassemble their work at another location to stay a step ahead of the government.[26] Ashcroft, however, clearly took notice of the amendment, and its surprising passage helped spur his national tour.

An internal Justice Department investigation in 2003 revealed dozens of cases in which department employees had been accused of serious civil rights and civil liberties violations, and this did not help Ashcroft's defense of the act. The Office of Inspector General found thirty-four credible reports of violations, including charges that Arab and Muslim immigrants in federal detention centers had been beaten. A federal prison doctor received a reprimand for telling an inmate during a physical exam, "If I was in charge, I would execute every one of you" because of "the crimes you all did." In another case, investigators said they were still exploring the allegation that a corrections officer had ordered a Muslim inmate to take off his shirt "so the officer could use it shine his shoes."[27] Critics on both sides of the partisan fence pointed to the report as evidence that the government was overstepping its bounds, using the USA Patriot Act as license for a broad range of activities that stretched—or broke—the bounds of civil rights and civil liberties.

Public opinion polls produced a cloudy picture of the political situation. Ashcroft trumpeted a July 2003 poll by Fox News/Opinion Dynamics in which 91 percent of respondents believed that the act had not affected their civil rights or those of a family member.[28] However, a 2003 poll on the second anniversary of the September 11 attacks showed that 34 percent of those responding were "very concerned" and another 32 percent were "somewhat concerned" that new measures to fight terrorism could restrict individual freedom.[29] The differing poll results showed several things, including the fact that most Americans knew relatively little about what the USA Patriot Act provided, so how individuals responded depended heavily on how pollsters asked their questions. However, the polls also showed a significant level of anxiety among Americans that the act and the broader war on terrorism contained potential threats to civil rights and civil liberties.

Critics focused on a handful of the act's provisions, especially the sneak-and-peek authority, which allowed federal authorities far more flexibility to act in secret, without informing the targets of their investigation about searches of their homes and property. Critics worried about how broadly the law might be applied—how many innocent nonterrorists might find their property searched without any knowledge of it. In addition, those opposing the act criticized the "tangible thing" provision, which allowed federal authorities to examine financial, library, travel, video rental, religious, phone, and medical records. Like the sneak-and-peek provision, it not only allowed federal officials broader authority to look at records, but it also let them keep these investigations secret. Some people remarked that although the act supposedly did not allow someone's records to be searched simply because he or she had written an article criticizing the Patriot Act, they wondered if the act's language would be interpreted differently if the author was from an Arab country.[30] No public notice meant no accountability for such searches. How often they were undertaken, and for what reasons, would simply be unknown.

In Ashcroft's counterattack, he contended that the Patriot Act merely extended to terrorist cases investigative techniques that federal officials had been using for years against organized crime figures. He stated that the act had proven an important tool in helping federal, state, and local officials to connect the dots and improve coordination. The attorney general pointed to the indictment of Sami al-Arian, charged with having financial ties to the Palestinian Islamic Jihad, a terrorist organization responsible for murdering more than one hundred people. The group's victims included Alisa Flatow, who died in a bus bombing in Gaza. Her father said, "When you know the resources of your government are committed to right the wrongs committed against your daughter, that instills you with a sense of awe. As a father you can't ask for anything more."[31]

Ashcroft's Web site in support of the act said that it had "assisted us in obtaining the indictment by enabling the full sharing of information and advice about the case among prosecutors and investigators."[32] In defending the act's value, the Justice Department pointed to the breakup of terrorist cells in Buffalo, Detroit, Seattle, and Portland. Half of al Qaeda's senior leaders had been captured or killed, and "more than 3,000 operatives have been incapacitated." Justice officials said that as of late 2003, 143 individuals had been convicted or had pleaded guilty. That list included shoe bomber Richard Reid, who had tried to bring down the American Airlines jet from Paris; John Walker Lindh, the "American Taliban" captured by American troops in Afghanistan; six members of the Buffalo cell, who were convicted and decided to cooperate with investigators; two members of the Detroit cell; and Iyman Faris, who pleaded guilty in a plot to blow up the Brooklyn Bridge. "We have expanded freedom over the past two years while protecting civil liberties and protecting people here and around the world from further terrorist attacks," the department claimed.[33]

President Bush, in fact, used the second anniversary of the terrorist attacks to ask for even greater federal powers in a new version of the Patriot Act. The 2001 law, he said, gave investigators important new ammunition in the war against terrorism, but it did not go far enough. He asked Congress to "untie the hands of our law enforcement officials" by giving them stronger power to investigate and detain terrorism suspects. "Under current federal law, there are unreasonable obstacles to investigating and prosecuting terrorism, obstacles that don't exist when law enforcement officials are going after embezzlers and drug traffickers," he told an audience at the FBI Academy. "For the sake of the American people, Congress should change the law and give law enforcement officials the same tools . . . to fight terror that they have to fight other crime."[34] In particular, Bush asked that federal law enforcement agencies be permitted to issue "administrative subpoenas," which would allow officials to investigate individuals without obtaining advance approval from a judge or a grand jury. In addition, he proposed laws expanding the federal death penalty to more crimes and making it more difficult for suspected terrorists to be released on bail. "If we can use these subpoenas to catch crooked doctors," Bush said, "the Congress should allow law enforcement officials to use them in catching terrorists."[35]

Bush chose a particularly tough tactic to fight rising efforts in Congress and across the country to repeal portions of the USA Patriot Act. In part, Bush hoped to use the anniversary of the September 11 attacks to renew the fight for proposals, especially the highly contentious administrative subpoenas, which Congress had removed from the original bill. It was a strategy he had used well in pushing for big tax cuts: He had lobbied for large cuts in 2001, but the Democrats forced smaller cuts than those he originally proposed. Two years later, instead of retreating in the face of rising deficits, he fought for—and won—even more cuts. The administration tried the same strategy on homeland security. Instead of using Attorney General Ashcroft, who had become a lightning rod for complaints about violations of civil liberties, administration strategists put the president himself in the spotlight to make the proposal. "It's clear the administration, now on the defensive, is trying to use offense as a defensive strategy," charged the executive director of the ACLU, Anthony Romero.[36]

Rep. John Conyers Jr., the senior Democrat on the House Judiciary Committee, objected. "Removing judges from providing any check or balance on John Ashcroft's subpoenas does not make us safer, it only makes us less free. Of course terrorists should not be released on bail, but this administration has a shameful record of deeming law-abiding citizens as terrorists and taking away their rights," he said.[37] Many Republicans likewise were concerned about the new proposals. But with the president forcefully making the case, and with his speech on the anniversary of the attacks, they felt they had little choice but to remain quiet.

Nevertheless, the USA Patriot Act was a highly unusual piece of federal legislation. Rarely had any public policy issue united critics from both conservative and liberal ends of the political spectrum. On the right, condemnation came from those who had long worried that a strong government might hinder the exercise of individual freedom. On the left, opponents were concerned that innocent individuals would be swept up in the administration's zeal to fight terrorists. Critics from both sides quietly suggested that the administration was using the war against terrorism to promote new governmental powers that Congress had rejected in years past. No one argued for being soft on terrorists, and no one wanted to risk another big attack, but many involved felt that some kind of line had to be drawn in the shifting sand of homeland security legislation.

BALANCING SECURITY AND RIGHTS

While the debate raged, there was widespread disagreement on just where to draw this line between the stronger powers the government said it needed and the protections of civil rights and civil liberties that had, for many decades, been fundamental to American democracy. Having stood atop the pile of debris that once had been the World Trade Center, inhaling the pungent smoke and surrounded by determined rescue workers, President Bush had developed an unshakable commitment to making the country as safe as possible. Civil libertarians, conservatives and liberals alike, worried that the post–September 11 changes could transform American society. The USA Patriot Act and the president's proposals for a second, stronger version, they feared, could have as lasting an impact on the country as the American Revolution. This time, however, the legacy would be one of enduring restrictions on liberty, the opposite of the legacy of freedom established by the nation's founders. Both sides knew that the struggle was titanic. Rarely does a nation face such fundamental choices about its future.

The debate gained steam as the issue developed. Unlike most public policy controversies, in which debate peaks during the congressional battle over proposed legislation and then wanes with time, concern about the Patriot Act only grew following its passage. The number of state and local governments passing resolutions against it swelled. The confidence of critics—and the concern of Bush administration officials—increased, in part because of what now appeared to be legitimate worry that in the weeks after September 11 high emotions had led Congress to pass the measure too quickly, without careful examination. As the act's details became clearer, they stirred up more worry. Moreover, as the immediate effects of September 11 faded slightly, so did concern about another imminent attack, and concerns about the threat to traditional liberties grew. Reports such as the one about the imprisonment of children at Guantanamo and the complaints of the librarians motivated critics to ask what the administration truly had in mind. The second wave of Bush administration proposals led both members of Congress and civil liberties activists to dig in for what they expected would be a protracted battle.

The battles proved surprisingly dynamic. New problems continued to appear, which forced the administration to rethink its strategy. In 2003, just before the second anniversary of the September 11 attacks, a homesick man, Charles McKinley, managed to have himself shipped inside a crate, by air freight, from New York to Dallas. Government officials worried whether his strange case demonstrated a need to restrict civil rights and increase scrutiny of air cargo even further. McKinley had had the $550 price billed to the warehouse where he worked. He packaged himself inside the small crate, addressed it to his parents in Texas, and had himself picked up. The plane made stops in Niagara Falls, New York, and Fort Wayne, Indiana, before landing in Dallas. McKinley's adventure went completely unnoticed until the crate arrived at his parents' home. The deliveryman removed it from the truck to wheel it to the front door and was stunned to see a pair of eyes peering at him from inside. McKinley broke the crate open and started to crawl out. The delivery driver called the police. Federal investigators looked into how he had managed to evade security, and late-night comedians had fabulous material. McKinley was lucky. He could have been stowed in the unpressurized area of the airplane and would quickly have died, but the air freight company's employees happened to put him instead inside the heated, pressurized part of the cabin. McKinley ended up in jail on unrelated traffic and bad-check charges—federal officials could not find any law under which to prosecute him for his adventure. But "[h]e violated the law of stupidity if nothing else," said district attorney Bill Hill.[38]

Every new occurrence like this one raised the question: Was the case a dangerous sign of a homeland security system full of holes, which required tighter rules and more careful government scrutiny? Or was it evidence that people can sometimes do very stupid things without fundamentally endangering anyone else? Homeland security continued to generate new puzzles for civil rights that constantly raised the old questions, surrounded by new uncertainties. Consider these cases:

- *Screening grandmothers and babies.* Many of the airline security system's critics complained that security officials were needlessly delaying and scaring older travelers and small babies who were unlikely to pose a terrorist risk. Federal officials countered by pointing to a teddy bear seized at Orlando International Airport that screeners discovered contained a loaded .22 caliber derringer. An Ohio family of five was returning home after a Florida vacation. During the x-ray process, screeners found a small hole at the bottom of the toy. They discovered that the bear contained a pistol stolen in 1996 from a home in Barstow, California. Family members said that someone had given the bear to the child two days earlier at an Orlando hotel. After questioning them, federal officials sent the family back home. Screeners also picked up a man who had slid a knife down the back of a six-year-old child's shirt and another man, aged sixty-seven, who had concealed a nine-inch knife inside a hollowed-out prosthetic leg. TSA spokesman Robert Johnson pointedly said, "We are criticized a lot for screening grannies and babies: 'Why are they checking this? My two-year-old isn't a terrorist.' This underscores the need to screen everyone and everything." Johnson concluded, "We can't allow terrorists any opportunity."[39]
- *Fake IDs converted to real driver's licenses.* Investigators from the U.S. General Accounting Office set out to assess the security of the nation's system for providing driver's licenses. After passports, the driver's license is the gold standard—it is the standard identification accepted at airport security checkpoints as well as the permit for driving a car. GAO investigators used regular desktop computers

and inexpensive, off-the-shelf software to create fictitious identification documents, such as driver's licenses, birth certificates, and Social Security cards, and tried to exchange them for real driver's licenses. At all eight of the motor vehicle departments where they tried—in Virginia, Maryland, South Carolina, the District of Columbia, Arizona, California, Michigan, and New York—they succeeded. "If the General Accounting Office can do this, obviously terrorists can do it," said Sen. Charles Grassley, R-Iowa.[40] GAO investigators also obtained valid Social Security numbers for two fictitious infants and used counterfeit documents to enter the United States from Jamaica, Barbados, Mexico, and Canada.[41]

- *Lax security at the back door.* Airplane travelers got used to long lines and heavy screening with increased airport security. Organizations representing flight attendants, however, complained that security was lax for airport workers, some of whom turned out to be illegal aliens. At many airports, employees only had to show an ID to enter and they received no screening. Cars and trucks rarely received inspection. Nearly a thousand construction workers at the Dallas–Ft. Worth airport entered the facility daily without any screening. Although airport officials said they had established tight controls, the International Association of Flight Attendants said only San Francisco and Denver had met federal standards for perimeter security.[42]

- *Color codes for air travelers.* The Transportation Security Administration was concerned that the computer system for identifying potentially dangerous airline passengers was not tight enough. It created a new, color-coded system to designate all passengers as green (90 percent of travelers), meaning that they would receive regular screening at check-in and the security checkpoint; yellow (8 percent of travelers), for those to receive additional screening; or red (1–2 percent of travelers) for those who would be barred from flying and might face arrest. The TSA would examine the flyer's personal background, criminal history, cities of departure and arrival, and traveling companions, how the person's ticket was purchased, and the date of ticket purchase. For example, someone who paid by cash at the last minute, or someone who bought a one-way ticket, might be subject to extra screening. The new Computer Assisted Passenger Pre-Screening System II would, a TSA official said, "provide new protections for the flying public." He added, "Not only should we keep passengers from sitting next to a terrorist, we should keep them from sitting next to wanted ax murderers." An official at the ACLU objected to the new system, saying, "This system is going to be replete with errors." In fact, "You could be falsely arrested. You could be delayed. You could lose you ability to travel."[43]

- *Asleep at the switch.* Flight attendants readying a plane in Pittsburgh for an early morning departure were understandably surprised to discover Louis Esquivel already aboard, sitting asleep in the seventh row. Esquivel said that he wanted to go to St. Louis and that he had taken a circuitous route around security to get aboard. He ducked behind a ticket counter, crawled along a baggage conveyor belt, pried open a door, got into a van whose keys were sitting in its ashtray, drove to the gate, and boarded the unlocked plane. Asked about the stunning breach of security, the head of security for the TSA said, "It raised tremendous alarms for me, and obviously, I'm pretty upset about it." [44]

- *Divulging personal information about a million travelers.* JetBlue Airways was highly embarrassed to confess that it had given personal information about more than one million of its passengers to a private company that was working under a contract to the Pentagon to try to develop a screening system to identify travelers who posed a high risk. Divulging the information had violated the company's own policies for safeguarding the privacy of its customers, and JetBlue's chief executive acknowledged, "This was a mistake on our part" and that "many of our customers feel betrayed by it." [45] The company scrambled to try to repair the damage to its reputation. Several months later, however, Northwest Airlines revealed that it, too, had violated its privacy policy by sharing data on millions of passengers with the federal government. The airlines struggled with how best to balance the search for security with the imperative for privacy.

"When dangers increase, liberties shrink. That has been our history, especially in wartime," explains Stuart Taylor Jr. Unquestionably, the nation must recalibrate the balance between liberty and security, but in determining how best to do so, Taylor argues, "We are also stuck in habits of mind that have not yet fully processed how dangerous our world has become or how ill-prepared our legal regime is to meet the new dangers." [46] This predicament proved especially devilish because the only way to know how low to set the security bar was to take a chance on an attack and risk the devastating consequences that could occur from miscalculation. After September 11, administration officials did not want to be in a position of having to defend themselves against charges that they failed to protect the nation ever again. They realized that there were risks to civil liberties in their approach, but they believed that they had to take those risks to secure the nation.

How could officials know whether they had gone too far? The absence of a terrorist attack might mean that the administration had calibrated its strategy just right, or simply that terrorists had changed their strategies and were planning something different. On the other hand, an attack could occur in the future because it is fundamentally impossible to protect everyone against everything all of the time. Even seemingly absurd and paranoid government restrictions on civil rights and civil liberties might not necessarily defend against all terrorist threats. It is impossible ever to know where best to set the balance—safety is no guarantee that the government did not go too far, and attack is not necessarily a sign that the government did not go far enough. As cases challenging the USA Patriot Act and the Bush administration's strategy of detaining prisoners in Guantanamo began wending their way through the federal courts, even some early proponents began worrying that the policies had gone too far.

Thus, homeland security is about setting a balance. Where that balance is set must ultimately be a political judgment, made by political officials through the rough-and-tumble debates of the political process. The tough and sometimes nasty battles over the USA Patriot Act in many ways represent the process at its best. With the nation tiptoeing into new problems it had never faced before, it needed to devise untested policies to solve uncertain issues. To make the problem even more devilish, it was one in which citizens, quite rightly, expected their public officials to provide them protection and safety in their homes and workplaces—as well as freedom and liberty in their daily lives.

7

Stress Test

How does the American political system respond to big shocks? The American people naturally want the government to escape such shocks as much as possible. But when they happen—as indeed they will—we insist that the system be able to weather them as well as possible. Americans have long treasured their civil rights and civil liberties, including our ability to travel without restriction and work at jobs of our choice. We appreciate being able to relax and enjoy our free time. We expect the government to provide basic services without imposing exorbitant taxes. Americans would not want these and other treasured values and freedoms to be sacrificed as the government seeks to right itself after a big shock. The aftermath of September 11, 2001, was no exception. Government officials pledged that the terrorists would not win and that American principles would be preserved. At the same time, public officials promised to do everything possible to prevent such attacks from occurring again, even if that meant imposing limits (if only temporary ones) on some of those same principles. Their job was to determine what was wrong with the system and how the horrific September 11 attacks had come to pass.

Just like a cardiologist's stress test, the September 11 attacks served an important diagnostic function. What can be done to ensure that such attacks do not occur and, if they do, that loss of life and damage are minimized? Such a stress test helps identify the deep and enduring behavioral patterns of government agencies, programs, and officials. It defines which parts of the political system work well, which do not, and what—if anything—can be done to fix those that do not make the grade. It can help identify the system's instincts and reactions, the elements that unexpectedly loom up and take precedence, and perhaps those expected issues that fail to materialize.

OPENING THE POLICY WINDOW

In his classic *Agendas, Alternatives, and Public Policies,* John Kingdon theorizes that from time to time "policy windows" open that allow new issues to move onto the nation's agenda. For policy change to occur, an issue has to ripen, wait for a policy window to open, and then leap through. "Policy windows open infrequently, and do not stay open long," Kingdon explains.[1] The terrorist attacks did more than pop open a window—they blew down a wall, and through the resulting hole came a raging stream of policy proposals. A truly remarkable range of issues tried to squeeze through the "homeland security" window. The Bush administration used it to strengthen its case for war in Iraq. The travel industry, from theme parks to airlines, claimed it lost millions when frightened Americans refused to travel. Sales at some major retailers slipped, and large corporations invested in new private security systems. Local governments posted guards at power plants and bridges, and state governments conducted new bioterror drills. Private companies rushed a wide variety of new products to store shelves, and old products like duct tape and plastic sheets unexpectedly found new markets. Lobbyists across the country had long lists of things they wanted the government to do. For interests that somehow could fashion their cases into some form of "homeland security," the September 11 attacks provided an unparalleled opportunity to obtain action.

The nature of the homeland security problem multiplied the opportunities for action. Terrorism can emerge unexpectedly from any of a considerable number of sources, with a stunning array of consequences. The huge impact of the terrorist attacks created a demand for strong leadership. But the breadth and ambiguity of the problem made it impossible to decide *which* action was *most* needed. The airlines quickly won their bid for financial support. Aid to state and local governments came much more slowly. The Bush administration implicitly linked September 11 with Saddam Hussein but later backed away from the connection when evidence failed to materialize. But all of these issues—and many more—tried to crawl through the policy window that Kingdon describes.

Policy windows like the September 11 attacks open rarely in part because few shocks are likely to be so large and in part because of the nature of terrorism. As analyst Robert Kupperman told Congress two years to the day before the attacks, "The problem with terrorism is its episodic nature. During the periods of relative calm, large governments, including our own, view terrorism as a minor annoyance, especially when compared with grander visions of geopolitics, and it is often difficult to get the policy levels of government focused on the problem at all. But when an incident occurs, particularly one dominated by media coverage, terrorism takes on virtual strategic significance. When terrorists strike, governments go on hold, paralyzed by an unfolding human drama which is televised for all to see."[2] New problems intrude and old ones reemerge.

So just what kind of problem is homeland security—and what must we do to solve it? Like all other policy problems, it does not have an absolute definition. Individuals see and interpret events to fit their views of the world. Those interpretations in turn define what makes a problem a problem, and what kind of problem it becomes. In the eyes of sociologists, this is a "social construction of reality," a reality that has meaning as people see it. That also means that individuals come to "own" specific problems. Those involved in the policy process struggle not only to determine what "reality" means but who is in the best position to advance it.[3] As a result, Christopher J. Bosso argues, conflict frequently emerges "over whose alternative construction of reality will stick. But none of this takes place in a vacuum."[4] As an issue, homeland security has a vast array of aspects. They have rippled through the policy system, with many key players struggling to define the term to their advantage and competing to take advantage of the policymaking opportunities that the September 11 attacks created:

- *Defense strategy.* America's military forces grew out of the cold war era and the need to counter large, nuclear-equipped Soviet forces. The wars in Afghanistan and Iraq confirmed the need for a lighter and swifter military force, equipped to move into Afghani mountains or Iraqi deserts and fight guerilla and nomadic opponents. This did not mean abandoning the traditional American military force structure, but it did mean restructuring it to make it more flexible. In pursuing that strategy, Bush's defense secretary, Donald Rumsfeld, found himself engaged in constant controversy within his own department as military analysts debated how best to configure the military for fighting terrorism while protecting the nation for more conventional threats.

- *Intelligence collection and integration.* "Connecting the dots" became the catchphrase following the attacks. Everyone agreed on the need to link both the collection and analysis of intelligence more effectively. Several years after the attacks, the FBI's operations had fundamentally changed, even though shifting the agency's traditional catch-and-convict culture proved difficult. Indeed, the Justice Department's own inspector general found that, two years after the September 11 attacks, the bureau had not yet developed a comprehensive system for coherently processing all of the intelligence it received from other agencies. Its information technologies were not capable of processing key intelligence and other pivotal data.[5] Despite improved intelligence-sharing efforts with other agencies, including the FBI, the CIA and NSA were still fighting to maintain their respective autonomy, and the Department of Homeland Security's role in intelligence was unclear. Linking the intelligence agencies was difficult, progress was slow, and the process is ongoing.

- *Border security.* Shocked by the ease with which the terrorists had penetrated American society, policymakers determined to do far better at keeping potential terrorists and their weapons out. The nation's long borders and the massive number of seaborne containers it used in international commerce made this a thankless and fruitless task. Strategists quietly admitted that complete security was impossible. Their task was to determine which risks were greatest and how best to defend against them.

On March 18, 2003, Senior Border Patrol Agent Monica Monroy, part of the San Diego Sector Horse Patrol unit of the U.S. Department of Homeland Security, scanned pedestrians as they approached the border between the United States and Mexico. The start of the war with Iraq was imminent, and the department had raised the nation's alert status from yellow to orange. Border patrols like Monroy's were part of the tightened security procedures.

- *Immigration.* Almost since the opening of Ellis Island, the INS (now the Bureau of Citizenship and Immigration Services) had carried the reputation of being one of the federal government's most troubled agencies. Its computer systems were out of date, and upgrading them was an expensive and lengthy process. Foreign contractors sometimes staffed the visa-granting process in other countries, which made it harder to increase scrutiny of those who wanted to visit the United States. Other countries resisted U.S. demands for tougher screening and new passports that are harder to counterfeit and easier to scan into databases. Integrating these same databases proved another daunting job.
- *Aviation security.* The federal government took over control of the airport security from private contractors and considerably tightened the screening of passengers boarding airplanes. Analysts quickly realized, however, that no process was perfect. They also pointed to other holes in the system, from the screening of checked bags and the shipment of air cargo to the security of airport perimeters and the screening of airport workers. News reports pointed to a seemingly endless stream of possible vulnerabilities. Determining which risks were genuine— and which of these were most important—proved a continual struggle.

- *Strengthening first responders.* Everyone agreed that the homeland defense system was only as strong as the local officials who answered the first call. Asked to stretch the limits of the traditional "all-risk" strategy to encompass new and unprecedented scenarios, local officials complained that they remained overstretched and underresourced.

HOW DOES THE POLITICAL SYSTEM REACT TO STRESS?

For students of public policy, a central question is whether big stresses such as the terrorist attacks of September 11 leave the political system deeply rooted in its usual pattern of incremental change or whether it sparks something greater, more sudden, and more profound. In the early 1970s, paleontologist Stephen Jay Gould examined just this question in trying to explain the evolution of life. Scientists had long argued, in the tradition of Charles Darwin, that environmental forces pressed plants and animals to adapt to new circumstances. Those that adapted most successfully were those that endured; those that did not slipped away. Evolution was thus a relatively steady course.

Together with his colleague Niles Eldredge, Gould stunned the world of biology by arguing that evolution often took a very different, very unanticipated course. Darwinian theory predicted that scientists ought to find a series of fossils that charted the incremental steps taken by organisms as they evolved. However, when researchers looked for those in-between fossils, they often could not find them. Were they looking in the wrong places? Not looking carefully enough? Or could it be, as Gould and Eldredge concluded, that the in-between creatures did not exist? The pair became convinced, in fact, that life changes not so much through *evolution* as through *revolution,* not so much through gradual adaptation as via the effects of catastrophic events, such as meteor strikes. Big forces, they argued, periodically produce big transformations.[6]

If we want to understand the truly important forces shaping life, Gould maintained, we have to understand that life exists in a relatively steady equilibrium most of the time, punctuated occasionally but importantly by radical change: "Punctuational change writes nature's primary signature."[7] From this came his theory of "punctuated equilibrium," which shook paleontology to its core. For Gould, the long tableaus of incremental change are not nearly as interesting or pivotal as the short but hugely important bursts of fundamental change that, in turn, dramatically reshape the evolution of life.

Frank R. Baumgartner and Bryan D. Jones have suggested that similar patterns exist for public policy problems. They contend that the political system is relatively stable most of the time, with change occurring incrementally. However, forces tend to build and then to erupt explosively in large, fundamental change when big events roil the political system. "Important political questions are often ignored for years," but sometimes everyone focuses on the same issues in the same ways. As attention surges, so does the pressure for policy change. As a result, "external shocks" periodically shift public debate and public policy.[8] "Punctuated equilibrium, rather than stability and immobilism, characterizes the American political system."[9]

The Baumgartner and Jones argument proved just as contentious in political science as Gould's did in paleontology. Just as Gould attacked the dominant idea of his field, Baumgartner and Jones countered the time-honored and timeworn orthodoxy of American politics. Charles E. Lindblom had laid part of the foundation for the pair's theory a half-century earlier with his famous article "The Science of 'Muddling Through,'" in which he contended that "incrementalism" not only described the way most things happened most of the time, but also was the way they *should* happen. Incrementalism, he argued, provided a self-adjusting process of correcting little mistakes before they became big ones.[10] Aaron Wildavsky echoed Lindblom's ideas with his study of the federal budget process. He concluded that policymakers set most agencies' budgets most of the time by making small, "fair-share" incremental adjustments to each agency's existing base. Like Lindblom, he concluded that this provided not only a good description of most budgetary decisions but also a good normative prescription for how things should operate.[11]

Neither theory defines clearly how large a change must be to qualify as "incremental" or the length of time over which an equilibrium might be "punctuated." In the short term, most changes can appear incremental; over the long run, new equilibriums emerge. The real issue, however, is how big a change is and how fast it transforms policy—whether the complex forces within the political system provide a braking action and an impetus toward incrementalism or whether major shocks such as the September 11 attacks do indeed punctuate the old equilibrium and push the system to deep and fundamental changes. Should we expect to see, as Lindblom suggests, a string of fossils suggesting a gradual evolution of the U.S. political system? Or will we discover occasional large breaks in the chain of fossils that suggest big shocks that produced big changes?

As important as this question is, there is still a deeper one. When the system changes, what forces operate within it to shape the reaction? Just as in the cardiologist's stress test, an important value of analyzing the results of stress is to discover the system's underlying forces. We are not only interested in the size and rate of the system's change, but what prompts it to move and what holds it back.

Reading the Stress Test

When cardiologists assess a patient's stress tests, they carefully examine the tracings produced by the heart monitors, which show how the heart reacted to the stress. They check the heart's rhythms, how much the test's stress accelerated the

Figure 7.1 Incrementalism

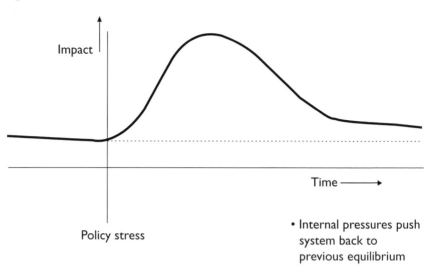

Impact

Time ⟶

Policy stress

• Internal pressures push system back to previous equilibrium

heart rate, whether the stress produced potentially dangerous reactions, and how well the heart settled back to a normal rhythm when the treadmill slowed down.

What would we see if we had similar tracings to record the performance of the U.S. government in the aftermath of the huge September 11 stress test? Despite the advances in public opinion polling, scientists have not yet figured out a way to hook electrodes up to the body politic and to the nation's political institutions. But we can imagine what the stress test might look like in different models of the U.S. political system.

Figure 7.1 illustrates the incremental model. It traces the system moving along its normal path—and then being shocked by enormous stress. The stress rocks the system, but all of the powerful cross-pressures that make incrementalism such an influential force soon pull the system back to normal. Changes occur—from shifts in airline screening to new cooperation between the FBI and CIA—but the fundamental forces shaping policy in the system ultimately drift back, more or less, to where they previously had been.

But is a shock as great as the terrorist attacks likely to leave the system relatively stable? The punctuated equilibrium model argues that this is precisely when big changes to government occur—and it would be hard to imagine a bigger punctuation. The stress shakes up the system. Public officials react by creating a new cabinet department, dramatically shifting priorities, and living the "everything has changed" mantra. As the system recovers from the shock, it moves into a new and very different equilibrium. Figure 7.2 charts what a punctuated equilibrium model for the stress test would look like.

Figure 7.2 Punctuated Equilibrium

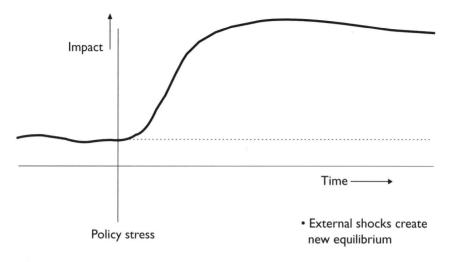

Which model better captures the results of the terrorism stress test? A careful look at the evidence presented in this book suggests that neither model is a good fit. On one hand, the events and aftermath of September 11 were distinctly non-incremental. The federal government engaged in the largest restructuring since the creation of the Department of Defense in 1947. Indeed, because all of the existing agencies maintained their existing missions and took on a new home-land security mission as well, the restructuring might well have been not only the largest but also the most difficult in U.S. history. New security arrangements completely transformed the airline industry. Airline passengers encountered new and unprecedented levels of screening, both visible and behind the scenes, that were unlikely to diminish. State and local governments found themselves pressed to guard a vast array of infrastructure. The FBI radically shifted the mission of most of its agents, from investigating crimes and arresting criminals after the fact to probing and disrupting possible terrorists before the fact. Enough major changes had irrevocably altered the nation. Never again could it settle back to the policies and practices it had known on September 10, 2001.

On the other hand, equally powerful forces put a brake on some of the changes. It proved difficult to sustain many of the new policies and practices in-stituted after the attacks. When long lines drove flyers away and increased the edginess of those preparing to fly, airlines soon pressured federal officials for changes in the passenger screening system. They resisted proposals to x-ray all checked baggage. In the intelligence arena, the one area in which everyone agreed on the need to connect the dots, the FBI, CIA, and NSA successfully fought to retain their autonomy, even though improved coordination and cooperation was the mandate. Proposals to concentrate all intelligence gathering into a single agency died a quick death. The Department of Homeland Security, designed to be the federal government's center of operations, found itself a weak player in intelligence debates. For its part, Congress reinforced the fragmentation of the nation's homeland security system by failing to make any major change in its own organization and functioning, which guaranteed that much of the fragmentation in executive branch powers and politics would endure.

Therefore, while the terrorist attacks provided a major shock to the system and unquestionably produced permanent changes, there also were equally compelling forces that undermined proposals for other important changes. As a result, the U.S. government ended up substantially different than on September 10, but not nearly at a place such as the post–September 11 days suggested. Neither had it reached the place that many homeland security analysts believe it should have reached.

As so many experts concluded, terrorism on U.S. soil had deep and profound effects. Was it an event that would forever and fundamentally change politics in the United States? Or did it represent a momentary blip in a long-term, relatively stable policy system, in which age-old forces resisted change? In the immediate aftermath of the attacks, the consensus was that "everything has changed." Had it? How much? And how would we know? When will we know, if ever?

Answering these questions is difficult, but we can pose two scenarios to help us approach some answers. First, on September 10, 2001, what would we have predicted that the policy world would look like in the not-too-distant-future? In the years that followed, big changes emerged that we would not have predicted before the attacks occurred. Security at airports increased dramatically. Foreign policy shifted to a far stronger focus on terrorism. The risks of bioterrorism loomed far larger. Security around public buildings and facilities, from the White House and sports arenas to theme parks and nuclear power plants, increased greatly. These changes were large and seemingly permanent. They were big impacts far beyond what one would have expected before the terrorist attacks.

Second, on September 12, 2001, in the immediate aftermath of the attacks, what would we have predicted the policy world would look like in the next few years? In the hours, days, and weeks that followed the attacks, grim determination emerged from the nation's shock and grief. Everyone agreed that everything *had* changed, and that the cracks in the system that permitted the attacks to occur *would* be filled. Just what would be done was unclear, but it was impossible to escape the sense of resolve.

In the years that followed, results exceeded what we once may have expected but fell short of the early promises. In early 2003, the TOPOFF exercise in Chicago and Seattle provided one of the first tests of the nation's emergency response system for terrorist attacks. The conclusion, according to the government's own report, was that the nation was not much better prepared to deal with a big terrorist attack than before September 11. "Fortunately, this was only a test," the report stated. The exercise revealed massive confusion and continuing problems in coordination and that "if a real incident occurs before final procedures are established, such unnecessary confusion will be unacceptable." Obstacles remained to coordinating the local response with federal intelligence. Almost no one could track the government's color-coded warning system and how it applied to the communities in the exercise. The result, the report found, was widespread disagreement and confusion about who was supposed to do what. One government observer commented, "The criticisms are among the worst I've ever heard." [12] Several years after September 11, the homeland security system continued to show dangerous vulnerabilities and problems of coordination. Despite the overwhelming consensus for action and the pressure for change, the system had proved surprisingly resistant to the fundamental restructuring that had seemed inevitable in the aftermath of the attacks.

To understand why the political system drifted to this new level—more vigilant than in the past, less transformed than might have been expected—requires charting the forces that produced this in-between response. What shaped the new equilibrium?

Homeland security, like all other important issues, does not exist in a vacuum. It has to fight for policy space with hurricanes and tornadoes, wars and health care, fires and murders, and the pressing need for child care. The system has built-in brakes that make it hard to sustain high-level attention on any one issue, no matter how important, for very long. Some of this is human nature; some is the inevitable flood of other policy problems that irresistibly demand attention. There is a natural tendency toward backsliding, toward resuming the previous equilibrium. When big stresses jar the system, it is never likely to retreat back completely to where it was, but neither can it maintain a laser-like focus on a single issue.

As a result, the system's stress test results are much more apt to look like Figure 7.3. Faced with a major shock, the system reacts quickly and forcefully, but it then tends to settle back to a new equilibrium—at a significantly different level than before (and thus unlike the incremental model) but not at the level that the punctuated equilibrium model would have suggested. It is more a case of *punctuated backsliding,* with a large initial jolt, a big change in policy, and a subsequent slip back toward the previous equilibrium. The result is an enduring pressure toward stasis in the system.

Pressures for Backsliding

What causes this backsliding? The stress test can also help us identify the forces pulling the system back from the "everything has changed" level. The pressures

Figure 7.3 Punctuated Backsliding

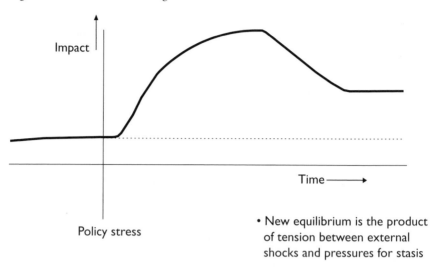

Impact

Time ⟶

Policy stress

• New equilibrium is the product of tension between external shocks and pressures for stasis

for backsliding came from four sources, which we have explored in earlier chapters: the bureaucracy's reaction to the many post–September 11 changes, the complexities of coordinating the nation's vast system of federalism, the recurring tendencies that bubbled up out of Congress, and the nature of the risk that terrorism presents (see Box 7.1).

The federal *bureaucracy* demonstrated its enduring instinct for autonomy. Although everyone recognized the need for greater coordination, most agencies resisted the idea of increasing coordination on another agency's terms. Coordination often becomes about turf—where the lines are drawn and who gets to call the shots. Strengthening coordination can mean shifting the bureaucratic balance of power, and this is something agencies quite understandably resist. The job is even harder when the agencies trying to coordinate have very different organizational cultures. The *what* of coordination is one thing; the *how* is quite another. Different agencies that approach problems from fundamentally different cultures can clash. For most agencies, including most of those within the new Department of Homeland Security, homeland security was not their only mission. Leaders became distracted by competing goals. The more time that passed after September 11, the more the older missions reasserted themselves and presented problems of balance to top officials. All of these forces combined to produce powerful pressures for backsliding.

The nation's system of *federalism* also challenges the mission of homeland security. Federal officials, of course, spend most of their time on federal issues. They certainly understand that the intergovernmental aspects of homeland security are

---

Box 7.1 Forces for Backsliding

- Bureaucracy
  - Instinct for autonomy
  - Different organizational cultures
  - Multiple, conflicting missions

- Federalism
  - Inattention by federal officials to state-local problems
  - Difficulties in state-local coordination
  - Difficulties coordinating among local governments

- Congress
  - Multiple, overlapping committee jurisdictions
  - Instinct to use homeland security funds for pork

- Nature of homeland security
  - Few rewards for preventing attacks
  - Recurring argument that money is more urgently needed elsewhere
  - Tendency for complacency to build over time

---

critical, but these often are not their most pressing concerns. It is little wonder, therefore, that state and local officials so often complain that federal officials have little understanding of the problems, both financial and policy, that they face. A Democratic Party task force on homeland security that surveyed 304 local government officials in late 2003 determined that 56 percent of those surveyed considered coordination with federal officials inadequate. Fifty-three percent believed that the Department of Homeland Security did not understand the vulnerabilities local governments faced, 87 percent believed that federal funding was inadequate, and 69 percent believed that the federal government was not doing everything it could to help.[13] (While the Democrats had been most interested in embarrassing the Bush administration, these findings matched the observations of many experts.) The recurring complaint that the federal government does not understand the needs of state and local governments is an old and enduring tension in the intergovernmental system. So, too, is the difficulty state governments have in securing better coordination among local governments and between state homeland security offices and local officials. The September 11 attacks sharpened these old strains and brought them painfully to the surface. The difficulty the system has in addressing them added to the pressures for backsliding.

Congress itself tended to increase the difficulties of coordination. Although Americans tend to look to the president as chief executive and the executive office to manage the government as a private executive would manage a company, the reality is that the bureaucracy is fundamentally the creature of Congress, not the president. Congress passes the laws, creates the programs, establishes the agencies, and appropriates the money. In the balance-of-power system, the president has a powerful role, but most of the time most federal agencies draw stronger influence from Capitol Hill. Even as members of Congress called on these agencies to connect the dots, Congress's own attention to homeland security remained remarkably fragmented. Congressional scholar Norman J. Ornstein counted thirteen House and Senate committees with at least some jurisdiction over homeland security, along with more than sixty subcommittees—eighty-eight committees and subcommittees in all.[14] Each carefully guarded its own jurisdictions. A new select committee on homeland security did not prove powerful enough to shake the deep congressional tradition of committees' tending their own jurisdictions. And for most members of Congress, the new funding for homeland security was more of an opportunity to bring cash back to their districts than to focus money on the areas of highest risk. The programs proved a meaty source of pork. Congress's procedures and operations contained built-in backsliding pressures, and it was impossible for federal agencies to coordinate their efforts if the congressional committees overseeing them did not.

The *nature of homeland security* adds a final backsliding pressure. There surely are strong incentives in the political system to punish anyone who might open the door to attack. The system reacts strongly to big stories that gain wide publicity—from the shoe bomber to the person who shipped himself as airborne freight—but the political system provides few rewards for *preventing* attacks. It is impossible to know for sure what attacks the system has prevented and what their consequences might have been. Thus it is hard to applaud successes, and success in preventing attacks always gets less publicity than dramatic cases of failure. Moreover, it is certain that resources invested in homeland security could have been invested instead in other policies, such as prescription drug benefits for senior citizens or more aid for college students. Thus, in the absence of attacks, it is easy to argue that other programs need the money more. Homeland security has a built-in imbalance of incentives that makes it hard to sustain a high level of attention over time, and these forces further reinforce the tendency toward backsliding. Success, or at least the absence of attack, can breed complacency, and complacency can make it easier for other issues to push into the policy arena and nudge homeland security aside.

One notable exception to this trend was the capture of Saddam Hussein in late 2003. Alleged to have masterminded the use of biochemical weapons on thousands and to have stockpiled hundreds of such weapons, American troops literally unearthed Hussein from a small "spider hole" with little more than the clothes on his back. As images of the bedraggled and almost zombie-like former dictator were broadcast around the world, proponents of a no-holds-barred, no-tolerance policy on terrorism proclaimed victory. Here was proof that proper coordination between various intelligence agencies, adequate funding for sophisticated technology and highly trained manpower, and ever-present vigilance paid out tremendously high dividends. There is no room for complacency and backsliding when victory could be just waiting to be found. But the pressures for backsliding soon began to build again. With Hussein's capture, American anxiety over the Iraq war palpably eased and domestic policy issues began to bubble to the surface once more.

WHAT HAS HOMELAND SECURITY DONE TO THE POLICY SYSTEM?

In examining the political origins of U.S. social policy, Theda Skocpol observed, "As politics creates policies, policies also remake politics." [15] The homeland security debate unquestionably remade politics. For the Bush administration, intent on strengthening the presidency, even at the expense of Republicans in Congress if necessary, the war on terrorism helped shift the balance of power. Worried about their own prerogatives, members of Congress countered by pressing for the creation of a new department of homeland security. After fighting off the plan for nine months, President Bush finally gave in, but he insisted that the department fit his own image. Congress retained great influence over the bureaucracy, but the president's role in shaping policy unquestionably grew.

Within the executive branch, the Defense Department won new power and new weapons for more flexible military campaigns. To the horror of many public interest groups, Attorney General Ashcroft's Justice Department sought a new balance for civil rights and civil liberties, and Ashcroft found himself on the defensive in guarding his strategy. The FBI worked hard to change its stripes, while the CIA and NSA struggled equally hard to cooperate in sharing intelligence while maintaining their autonomy. The new Department of Homeland Security achieved notable successes, including progress toward streamlining the nation's immigration and customs functions and integrating emergency management into the homeland security system. But on the highest-profile issue, intelligence gathering and analysis, the department typically found itself on the sidelines. Meanwhile, the tug-of-war over turf reinforced one of Washington's most fundamental instincts: when in doubt, reorganize.

A deeper, more difficult issue was how much of the homeland security coordination problem was structural, requiring reorganization of the bureaucracy, and how much was a problem with the networks among the key players, which required improving their working relationships. The strategy of terrorists leads them to seek new points of vulnerability to maximize damage and surprise. A system that struggles to restructure itself in response to the last attack could unintentionally create new sources of vulnerability and fail to take the steps needed to plug the system's holes. Terrorism is often very fluid, shifting in form, strategy, and tactics as opportunities present themselves. Government needs to be lithe, quick, and supple to respond effectively. A kind of "bureaucratosclerosis," or hardening of the administrative arteries. A single-minded focus on coordination as a structural problem could further choke the bureaucratic arteries and make it even more difficult for the system to adapt and respond to the dangers that terrorism presents.

Congress, in particular, demonstrated its oft-repeated pattern of fixing problems by changing organizational structure and appropriating money. In the case of a problem such as homeland security, where constantly shifting problems defied pigeonholing and where it was difficult to assess which problems were the most important places to spend money, Congress constantly risked being out of sync with the policy debate.

State and local governments found themselves in a profoundly paradoxical position. Each pointed to its respectively critical role as a first responder but complained that the new responsibilities had come without sufficient money. As state and local governments found themselves on the front lines of homeland security, they fumed that the federal government was not adequately sharing intelligence and guidance with its state and local partners. Sen. Diane Feinstein, D-Calif., put it flatly at a hearing discussing information sharing with state and local governments: "I can tell you gentlemen, the information does not flow." [16]

Both political parties have subtly sought to capitalize on the public's concerns and the other party's mistakes and in the process to exploit the political potential of being tough on terrorism. President Bush created lush visuals of his role as commander in chief, as when he landed on the aircraft carrier USS *Abraham Lincoln* to celebrate the end of the first phase of the Iraq war, which he linked to the global war on terrorism. A Hong Kong–based toy company capitalized on the event by producing a new action toy, "Elite Force Aviator: George W. Bush— U.S. President and Naval Aviator," a model of the president wearing a flight suit, retailing for $39.99. Soon thereafter, the Democrats countered with a "homeland security report card," which predictably was full of Cs, Ds, and Fs—with an overall grade of D.[17] Both parties realized that homeland security had the potential to be a realigning issue, shifting the balance of power between the parties, and both parties committed themselves to fight for the debate's high ground.

But both parties also realized that homeland security poses enormous political risk. There frequently is little political gain in *preventing* attacks. Citizens take for granted that their officials will try to keep the nation safe. There can be political risk if terrorist attacks occur, since the party in power can be blamed for failing to prevent them. At the same time, however, the September 11 attacks demonstrated that shocked citizens often rally around the flag and support a president who promises strong action. Terrorism's effects on the political system have proved deceptively difficult to forecast.

As Israel's decade-long experience shows, a sustained pattern of terrorist attacks can undermine the sitting government. After more than 375 Israelis died in clashes with Palestinians over a four-month period, Israel's voters in 2001 turned to a more conservative government, headed by Prime Minister Ariel Sharon. The Palestinian-Israeli conflict shows that terrorism can enhance the electoral chances of political candidates who take tough stands. On the other hand, the 2002 U.S. congressional midterm elections showed that candidates characterized as soft on defense can be at risk. Two Democratic senators—Missouri's Jean Carnahan and Georgia's Max Cleland—lost their seats in part because Republicans capitalized on the fact that they opposed the creation of the new Homeland Security Department. An ad attacking Cleland showed him, Saddam Hussein, and Osama bin Laden and charged that Cleland had voted against the creation of the department eleven times. The ad neglected to mention that Cleland had pushed for the Democratic version of the department before the president made his own proposal. So controversial that it was pulled after only airing a few days, it still cast the senator's patriotic vigor in a dim enough light to contribute to his loss, even though Cleland had lost an arm and both legs as a company commander in Vietnam.

The effects of the September 11 attacks reached virtually every corner of the American political system in some fashion, and they are unlikely to diminish. Indeed, it is unlikely that the nation can ever truly "win" the war against terrorism. We can never be fully secure, and it is likely that the campaign against terrorism will last decades. It is not a war that the federal government can fight on its own. Rather, it will be a campaign that will require strong and sustained partnerships among the nation's federal, state, and local governments, between government and the private sector, and between the United States and the world community. It is a war with large and uncertain costs that will compete with other national goals, like good education for children, sound retirement benefits for the elderly, and effective health care for everyone. It is one thing to fight a short campaign to change the government of a tyrant, as the United States did in Iraq in 2003. It is quite another to shift national goals, resources, strategies, and tactics to carry on a sustained effort to protect the nation from new, insidious, and clever terrorists. As the Gilmore Commission, a special advisory panel to the president and Congress, concluded in its 2003 report, *Forging America's New Normalcy:*

> There will never be an end point in America's readiness. Enemies will change tactics, citizens' attitudes about what adjustments in their lives they are ready to accept will evolve, and leaders will be confronted with legitimate competing priorities that will demand attention. . . . In the end, America's response to the threat of terrorism will be measured in how we manage the risk. There will never be a 100% guarantee of security for our people, the economy, and our society. We must resist the urge to seek total security—it is not achievable and drains our attention from those things that can be accomplished.

The "new normalcy," the report concludes, requires that the nation devise a strategy for pursuing its enduring values, reducing fear, and countering the terrorist threat.[18]

After September 11, the United States found itself embroiled in broad and contentious global issues that it could neither escape nor fully control. Defense analysts in the 1990s wondered how the fall of the Berlin Wall and the end of the cold war would affect diplomacy and the world order. They discovered that ethnic conflicts and terrorism have replaced tensions between the United States and the Soviet Union—that asymmetric conflicts have replaced symmetric ones. President Bush announced a strategy of preemption, which defined a military strategy in which the United States stood ready to launch an attack to prevent other forces from striking the nation. His critics contended that the go-it-alone strategy risked alienating the United States from its allies and undermining its ability to build international coalitions in the antiterror war. In a host of areas, the nation found itself facing new puzzles, with sweeping implications for policy and politics.

I know several experts on homeland security. Two things strike me about them. One is that they are very, very smart. They have an uncommon ability to sort through the vast noise and confusion of the homeland security debate to bring real clarity to the issues, which is no mean feat. The other is that they spend their time strategizing about events that most of us would gladly not think about. The very nature of asymmetric conflict—the focus on small forces strategically placed to bring maximum damage to large, powerful nations—is that it is uncertain, dangerous, and often aimed at innocents. The rise of new, post–cold war problems coupled with the rise of asymmetric conflict means that, unfortunately, they are unlikely to run out of work. The implications are sobering.

Can the American system cope with these ongoing challenges? The debate rages. Optimists, like Baumgartner and Jones, believe that the government and its institutions have tremendous flexibility to respond to shocks. Government, they claim, often makes its biggest and most productive changes when big events punctuate the equilibrium, and the system's resiliency gives it the ability to adapt. But other analysts are not so sure. John E. Chubb and Paul E. Peterson argue that government has steadily become less effective. Special interests steer policy away from the public interest. Congress is more fragmented, and the presidency is more politicized. The federal bureaucracy has become more labyrinthine and difficult to control. Efforts to tackle previous problems have often been unsuccessful. The roots of the problem, Chubb and Peterson say, are in the behavior of American political institutions.[19] Although they published their book in 1989, there is scant evidence that the nation has made much progress in resolving these issues. Debates about the performance of American government, if anything, have become more intense.

For some problems, such as the budget deficit or the balance of trade, the implications might be huge, but the immediate costs of failure—or even a stumble in dealing with the issues—are not catastrophic. For homeland security, however, even small errors can have huge and punishing effects. As homeland security rises as an issue, it collides with fundamental questions about whether American government can govern. The September 11 attacks revealed glaring holes. The nation's efforts since offer considerable hope as well as pointed warnings that the nation remains vulnerable. No one wants to discover these vulnerabilities through further shocks to the system. As cardiologists always tell their patients after a stress test, it is important to learn from the tracings of such tests and find ways of improving the system's ability to respond.

Notes

Chapter 1

1. CNN.com, "Forests of Columns Kept Building Standing," January 24, 2003, www.cnn.com/2003/US/01/24/attacks.pentagon/index.html.

2. "The Story of 'Let's Roll' " (2000–2001), www.letsrollheroes.com/thestory.shtml).

3. "The War Against America: An Unfathomable Attack," *New York Times*, September 12, 2001, A26.

4. Indira A. R. Lakshmanan, "Attack on America/Nations Respond," *Boston Globe*, September 12, 2001, sec. A.

5. David Saltonstall, "Terrorist Attack Rocks the Nation," *New York Daily News*, September 12, 2001, 6.

6. David Frum, *The Right Man: The Surprise Presidency of George W. Bush* (New York: Random House, 2003), 128.

7. David Saltonstall, " 'The Nation Sends Its Love,' " *New York Daily News,* September 15, 2001, 4.

8. Quoted in Edward Walsh, "Bush Encourages N.Y. Rescuers," *Washington Post,* September 15, 2001, A10.

9. Elisabeth Bumiller, "Two Strangers, Bush and New York City, Meet and Embrace in Calamity's Wake," *New York Times*, September 15, 2001, A6.

10. Ibid.

11. Address to a Joint Session of Congress and the American People, U.S. Capitol, Washington, D.C., September 20, 2001, available at www.whitehouse.gov.

12. Frum, *The Right Man*, 136.

13. The White House, "Governor Ridge Sworn In to Lead Homeland Security," October 8, 2001, www.whitehouse.gov/news/releases/2001/10/20011008-3.html.

14. William Safire, "On Language: Homeland," *New York Times Magazine*, January 20, 2002, 12.

15. Johns Hopkins Center for Civilian Biodefense, Center for Strategic and International Studies, ANSER, and Memorial Institute for the Prevention of Terrorism, *Dark Winter: Final Script*, June 22–23, 2001, at www.hopkins-biodefense.org/DARK%20WINTER.pdf.

16. Tara O'Toole, Michael Mair, and Thomas V. Inglesby, "Shining Light on 'Dark Winter,' " *Clinical Infectious Diseases* 34 (February 19, 2002): 972–983, www.journals.uchicago.edu/CID/journal/issues/v34n7/020165/020165.html.

17. Quoted at www.upmc-biosecurity.org/pages/events/dark_winter/dark_winter.html.

18. Eric V. Larson and John E. Peters, *Preparing the U.S. Army for Homeland Security: Concepts, Issues, and Options* (Santa Monica, Calif.: RAND, 2001), 1–2, www.rand.org/publications/MR/MR1251/.

19. Ibid.

20. Continuity of Government Commission, *Preserving Our Institutions—The First Report of the Continuity of Government Commission,* June 4, 2003, www.continuityofgovernment.org/pdfs/FirstReport.htm.

21. Fareed Zakaria, "The Politics of Rage: Why Do They Hate Us?" *Newsweek,* October 15, 2001, 22.

22. "Portraits of Grief," *New York Times,* www.nytimes.com/pages/national/portraits/.

Chapter 2

1. ABCNEWS.com, "The Cell," August 16, 2002, http://abcnews.go.com/sections/2020/DailyNews/wtc_yearTheCell_excerpt.html.

2. CBSNEWS.com, "From the Doomed Cockpits," October 16, 2001, www.cbsnews.com/stories/2001/10/16/archive/main314846.shtml.

3. Ricardo Alonso-Zaldivar, "Policy of Knives on Airplanes Being Re-Examined," *Los Angeles Times,* September 15, 2001, A20.

4. CNN Correspondent Susan Candiotti, *CNN Sunday Morning,* September 15, 2002, at www.cnn.com/TRANSCRIPTS/0209/15/sm.07.html.

5. CNN, "Maryland Police Release Hijacker Traffic Stop Video," January 8, 2002, http://edition.cnn.com/2002/US/01/08/inv.hijacker.video/.

6. CBSNEWS.com, "Hijackers Remain Mysterious," September 11, 2002, www.cbsnews.com/stories/2002/09/11/september11/main521523.shtml.

7. Described in a memo from FBI agent Colleen Rowley to FBI director Robert Mueller, May 21, 2002, www.time.com/time/covers/1101020603/memo.html.

8. Sen. Chuck Grassley, "Fixing the FBI," June 7, 2002, http://grassley.senate.gov/cgl/2002/cg02-06-7.htm.

9. Joint Inquiry Staff, Joint Committee on Intelligence, Congress of the United States, "Joint Inquiry Staff Statement—Part I," September 18, 2002, http://i.cnn.net/cnn/2002/ALLPOLITICS/09/18/intelligence.hearings/intel.911.report.pdf.

10. Brian Friel, "State Department Official Blasts Intelligence Agencies," *GovExec.com,* October 12, 2001, www.govexec.com/dailyfed/1001/101201b2.htm.

11. Federation for American Immigration Reform, "World Trade Center and Pentagon Terrorists' Identity and Immigration Status," April 2003, www.fairus.org/html/04178101.htm.

12. U.S. General Accounting Office, *Information Technology: Terrorist Watch Lists Should Be Consolidated to Promote Better Integration and Sharing,* Report GAO-03-322, April 23, 2003, "Highlights" page.

13. CNN.com, "Senators: 9/11 Report to Detail Intelligence Failures," July 24, 2003, www.cnn.com/2003/ALLPOLITICS/07/24/9.11.report/index.html.

14. U.S. Postal Service, "Message to Customers," October 17, 2001, www.usps.com/news/2001/press/pr01_1010tips.htm.

15. Marie McCullough, "Anthrax Hoaxes, False Alarms Taxing Authorities Nationwide," *Seattle Times*, November 10, 2001, http://seattletimes.nwsource.com/html/nationworld/134364704_angst10.html.

16. ABC News, "Nightline Biowar Series," October 1, 1999, http://abcnews.go.com/onair/Nightline/nl991001_biowar.html.

17. CNN.com, "One Year Later: Security Tighter, Cities Stretched," September 12, 2002, www.cnn.com/2002/US/09/06/prepared.cities.overview/index.html.

18. "The Shoe Bomber's World," *Time Online Edition*, February 16, 2002, www.time.com/time/world/article/0,8599,203478,00.html.

19. Susan Stellin, "There's No Tiptoeing Past Shoe Policy," *New York Times*, July 20, 2003, sec. 5, p. 8.

20. Tony Karon, "The 'Dirty Bomb' Scenario," *Time Online Edition*, June 10, 2002, at www.time.com/time/nation/article/0,8599,182637,00.html.

21. Harold Seidman, *Politics, Position, and Power: The Dynamics of Federal Organization*, 5th ed. (New York: Oxford University Press, 1998), 142. Portions of the material that follows originally appeared in "Contingent Coordination: Practical and Theoretical Problems for Homeland Security," *American Review of Public Administration* (2003).

22. Titan Systems Corporation, *Arlington County: After-Action Report on the Response to the September 11 Terrorist Attack on the Pentagon* (2002), A-4–A-7, www.co.arlington.va.us/fire/edu/about/pdf/after_report.pdf.

23. Ibid., 10.

24. Ibid., 9.

25. Ibid., 10

26. Ibid., 12–13.

27. Ibid., 10.

28. See McKinsey and Company, *Increasing FDNY's Preparedness* (2002), www.nyc.gov/html/fdny/html/mck_report/toc.html.

29. Ibid., 13.

Chapter 3

1. Alison Mitchell, "Joint Congress Transformed into a United Showcase of Courage and Resolve," *New York Times*, September 21, 2001, B5.

2. "President Bush's Address on Terrorism before a Joint Meeting of Congress," *New York Times*, September 21, 2001, B4.

3. Michael Taylor, "New Defense Office Takes Shape," *San Francisco Chronicle*, September 30, 2001, A21.

4. Chester I. Barnard, *The Functions of the Executive* (Cambridge: Harvard University Press, 1938), 94.

5. Sydney H. Freedberg Jr., "Homeland Defense Breaks Down Walls of Government," *GovExec.com*, October 19, 2001, www.govexec.com/dailyfed/1001/101901nj1.htm.

6. Ibid.

7. Herbert Emmerich, *Federal Organization and Administrative Management* (University: University of Alabama Press, 1971), 17.

8. For an exploration of this issue, see Robert Axelrod, *The Evolution of Cooperation* (New York: Basic Books, 1984), esp. 6–7; Joel D. Aberbach and Bert A. Rockman, "Mandates or Mandarins? Control and Discretion in the Modern Administrative State," *Public Administration Review* 48 (1988): 606–612; B. Dan Wood and Richard W. Waterman, "The Dynamics of Political Control of the Bureaucracy," *American Political Science Review* 85 (1991): 801–828; and Richard W. Waterman, Amelia Rouse, and Robert Wright, "The Venues of Influence: A New Theory of Political Control of the Bureaucracy," *Journal of Public Administration Research and Theory* 8 (January 1998): 13–38.

9. Dick Thornburgh, chairman, National Academy of Public Administration Panel on FBI Reorganization, Testimony before the Subcommittee on Commerce, State, Justice, the Judiciary, and Related Agencies, Committee on Appropriations, U.S. House of Representatives, June 18, 2003.

10. Gregory F. Treverton, "Set Up to Fail," *GovExec.Com*, September 1, 2002, www.govexec.com/features/0902/0902s6.htm.

11. Michael Fuoco, "Coast Guard Profile Higher on Rivers," *Pittsburgh Post-Gazette*, May 3, 2003, A1.

12. Statement of JayEtta Z. Hecker, General Accounting Office, *Coast Guard: Challenges During the Transition to the Department of Homeland Security*, Report GAO-03-594T, April 1, 2002, 2.

13. Anne M. Khademian, *Working with Culture: The Way the Job Gets Done in Public Programs* (Washington, D.C.: CQ Press, 2002), 3.

14. Interview with Michael O'Hanlon, *GovExec.com*, October 18, 2001, www.govexec.com/dailyfed/1001/101801njcom1.htm.

15. Robert Pear, "Traces of Terror: The New Department; Lawmakers Asking If Plan on Terror Goes Far Enough," *New York Times*, June 8, 2002, A1.

16. U.S. Department of Health and Human Services, *Accountability Report: Fiscal Year 2001* (Washington, D.C.: U.S. Government Printing Office, 2002), viii, www.hhs.gov/of/reports/account/acct01/pdf/intro.pdf.

17. Richard B. Schmitt, "FBI's Computer Upgrade Develops Its Own Glitches," *New York Times*, January 28, 2003, 1.

18. Shane Harris, "Rebooting the Bureau," *GovExec.com*, August 1, 2002, www.govexec.com/features/0802/0802s3.htm.

19. Schmitt, "FBI's Computer Upgrade."

20. Harris, "Rebooting the Bureau."

21. Kenneth A. Shepsle and Mark S. Bonchek, *Analyzing Politics: Rationality, Behavior, and Institutions* (New York: Norton, 1997), 359.

22. Geoff Earle and Mark Wegner, "Reorganization Plan Gains Bipartisan Support on Hill," *GovExec.com*, June 6, 2002, www.govexec.com/dailyfed/0602/060602cd1.htm.

23. Beryl A. Radin, *The Accountable Juggler: The Art of Leadership in a Federal Agency* (Washington, D.C.: CQ Press, 2002), 70.

24. James L. Sundquist, "Congress as Public Administrator," in *A Centennial History of the American Administrative State*, ed. Ralph C. Chandler (New York: Free Press, 1987), 285.

25. John Arquilla and David Ronfeldt, *Networks and Netwars: The Future of Terror, Crime, and Militancy* (Santa Monica, Calif.: RAND, 2001), ix.

26. Ibid., 364–365.

27. Brody Mullins and Pamela Barnett, "Move Underway to Authorize Homeland Security Office," *GovExec.com*, October 5, 2001, www.govexec.com/dailyfed/1001/100501cd1.htm.

28. Executive Order, October 8, 2001, www.whitehouse.gov/news/releases/2001/10/20011008-2.html.

29. Freedberg, "Homeland Defense Effort Breaks Down Walls of Government."

30. Patty Davis, "Critics Fault Airport Security System," CNN.com, September 18, 2001, http://edition.cnn.com/2001/TRAVEL/NEWS/09/18/rec.airport.security/.

31. George W. Bush, "Radio Address of the President to the Nation," October 27, 2001, www.whitehouse.gov/news/releases/2001/10/20011027.html.

32. April Fulton and Keith Koffler, "Senators Press House to Federalize Airport Security," *GovExec.com*, October 23, 2001, www.govexec.com/dailyfed/1001/102301cd2.htm.

33. CNN.com, "Daschle Joins Call for Independent 9/11 Probe," May 22, 2002, www.cnn.com/2002/ALLPOLITICS/05/22/probe.daschle/.

34. David Johnston and Neil A. Lewis, "Whistle-Blower Recounts Faults within the FBI," *New York Times*, June 7, 2002, A1.

35. Transcript of speech by President George W. Bush, *New York Times*, June 7, 2002, A20.

36. Ibid.

37. Kellie Lunney, "Administration Already Has Homeland Security Flexibility, Union Says," *GovExec.com*, August 28, 2002, www.govexec.com/dailyfed/0802/082802m1.htm.

38. Remarks by the President, Signing of Homeland Security Act, November 25, 2002, www.whitehouse.gov/news/releases/2002/11/20021125-6.html.

39. Siobhan Gorman, "FBI, CIA Remain Worlds Apart," *GovExec.com*, August 1, 2003, www.govexec.com/dailyfed/0803/080103nj1.htm.

40. John Gray, *Men Are from Mars, Women Are from Venus: A Practical Guide for Improving Communication and Getting What You Want in Your Relationships* (New York: HarperCollins, 1993); for the comparison, see Gorman, "FBI, CIA Remain Worlds Apart."

41. Gorman, "FBI, CIA Remain Worlds Apart."

42. "Homeland Security Department Targets Child Sex Abuse," *Washington Post*, July 10, 2003, A8.

Chapter 4

1. Tip O'Neill with Gary Hymel, *All Politics Is Local and Other Rules of the Game* (New York: Times Books, 1994).

2. Suzanne Goldeberg and Graham Usher, "Suicide Bomb Kills 16 Israelis in Hotel," *[London] Guardian Unlimited*, March 28, 2002, www.guardian.co.uk/israel/Story/0,2763,675293,00.html.

3. CBSNEWS.com, "Transcript: Postal Worker's 911 Call," November 7, 2001, www.cbsnews.com/stories/2001/11/07/archive/main317269.shtml.

4. This account is derived from Gerald M. Carbone, "The Miracle of Ladder 6 and Josephine," *Providence Journal*, September 11, 2002, www.projo.com/words/

st20021016.htm; and a report on *Dateline NBC*, "Miracle of Ladder Company 6," September 28, 2001.

5. Jonas, quoted by Dennis Cauchon and Martha T. Moore, "Miracles Emerge from the Debris," *USA Today*, September 6, 2002, www.usatoday.com/news/sept11/2002-09-05-miracles-usat_x.htm.

6. See, for example, Federal Emergency Management Agency, *A Nation Prepared: Federal Emergency Management Agency Strategic Plan, Fiscal Years 2003–2008* (Washington, D.C.: U.S. Government Printing Office, 2003), www.fema.gov/doc/library/text_reader_fema_strat_plan_fy03-08.doc.

7. Robbie Robinson, David A. McEntire, and Richard T. Weber, *Texas Homeland Defense Preparedness* (New York: Century Foundation, 2003), 28.

8. RAND Press Release, "Rand Study Finds Emergency Responders Believe They Have Inadequate Protection," August 20, 2003, www.rand.org/hot/press.03/08.20.html. See Tom LaTourrette, D. J. Peterson, James T. Bartis, Brian A. Jackson, and Ari Houser, *Protecting Emergency Responders, Volume 2: Community Views of Safety and Health Risks and Personal Protection Needs* (Santa Monica, Calif.: RAND, 2003).

9. Ibid., xxii; Donald F. Kettl, "The States and Homeland Security: Building the Missing Link" (New York: Century Foundation, 2003), www.tcf.org/publications/homeland_security/kettlpapers/Kettl.pdf.

10. Robinson, McEntire, and Weber, *Texas Homeland Defense Preparedness*, 19.

11. Dennis L. Dresang, "Strengthening Federal-State Relationships to Prevent and Respond to Terrorism: Wisconsin" (New York: Century Foundation, 2003), 13.

12. Warren B. Rudman, Richard A. Clarke, and Jamie F. Metzl, *Emergency Responders: Drastically Underfunded, Dangerously Unprepared* (Washington: Council on Foreign Relations, 2003), 1, 6, www.cfr.org/pdf/Responders_TF.pdf.

13. Portions of the discussion in this section originally appeared in Donald F. Kettl, "Contingent Coordination: Practical and Theoretical Problems for Homeland Security," *American Review of Public Administration* 33 (2003): 253–277.

14. T. Christensen and P. Laegreid, "Administrative Reform Policy: The Challenges of Turning Symbols into Practice" (paper presented at the Sixth National Public Management Research Conference, School of Public and Environmental Affairs, Indiana University, Bloomington, 2001).

15. Luther Gulick, "Notes on the Theory of Organization," in *Papers on the Science of Administration*, ed. L. Gulick and L. Urwick (New York: Institute of Public Administration, 1937), 1.

16. Ibid., 22.

17. Frederick W. Taylor, *Principles of Scientific Management* (New York: Harper and Brothers, 1911).

18. Robert Kanigel, *The One Best Way: Frederick Winslow Taylor and the Enigma of Efficiency* (New York: Viking, 1997).

19. Gulick, "Notes on the Theory of Organization," 23.

20. Christopher Hood, *The Art of the State: Culture, Rhetoric, and Public Management* (Oxford: Oxford University Press, 1998), 25.

21. The thrust of classical theory has been immersed in a major intellectual battle since the 1940s, with the structuralists getting the worst of it. See Robert A. Dahl, "The Science of Public Administration," *Public Administration Review* 7 (Winter

1947): 1–11; Herbert Simon, *Administrative Behavior: A Study of Decision-making Processes in Administrative Organization* (New York: Macmillan, 1947).

22. Gulick, "Notes on the Theory of Organization," 39.

23. Quoted by Robert Block, "FEMA Points to Flaws, Flubs in Terror Drill," *Wall Street Journal,* October 31, 2003, B1. See the report at Department of Homeland Security, "Top Officials (TOPOFF) Exercise Series: TOPOFF2—After Action Summary Report for Public Release," December 19, 2003.

24. Jo Becker, Sarah Cohen, and Spencer S. Hsu, "Anti-Terrorism Funds Buy Wide Array of Pet Projects," *Washington Post,* November 23, 2003, A1.

25. Ibid.

26. CNN.com, "Jeanne Meserve: Warnings Sparked Alert," February 8, 2003, www.cnn.com/2003/US/02/08/otsc.meserve/index.html.

27. Patricia A. Dalton, Testimony Before the Committee on Government Efficiency, Financial Management, and Intergovernmental Relations, Committee on Government Reform, U.S. House of Representatives, *Combating Terrorism: Intergovernmental Cooperation in the Development of a National Strategy to Enhance State and Local Preparedness,* Report GAO-02-550T, April 2, 2002; Richard Falkenroth, "The Problems of Preparedness: Challenges Facing the U.S. Domestic Preparedness Program," BCSIA Discussion Paper 2000-28, ESDP Discussion Paper ESDP-2000-05, John F. Kennedy School of Government, Harvard University (2000).

28. Federal Emergency Management Agency, Office of the Inspector General, *Semi-Annual Report: April 1, 2001–September 30, 2001* (2001), 9.

29. Falkenroth, "The Problems of Preparedness."

30. David Osborne, *Laboratories of Democracy: A New Breed of Governor Creates Models for National Growth* (Boston: Harvard Business School Press, 1988).

31. Alice Rivlin, *Reviving the American Dream: The Economy, the States and the Federal Government* (Washington: Brookings Institution Press, 1992), 31.

32. John Donahue, *Disunited States* (New York: Basic Books, 1997), 169.

Chapter 5

1. Railroad Commission of Texas, "Highway-Rail Grade Crossing Safety," www.rrc.state.tx.us/divisions/rail/gxovervw.html.

2. Martin Landau, "Redundancy, Duplication, and the Problem of Duplication and Overlap," *Public Administration Review* 29 (July-August 1969): 346–358.

3. See Todd LaPorte, "High Reliability Organizations: Unlikely, Demanding and At Risk," *Journal of Crisis and Contingency Management* 4 (1996): 55–59; Todd LaPorte and Craig Thomas, "Regulatory Compliance and the Ethos of Quality Enhancement: Surprises in Nuclear Power Plant Operations," *Journal of Public Administration Research and Theory* 5 (1996): 111–139; Todd LaPorte and Paula Consolini, "Working in Practice but Not in Theory: Theoretical Challenges of High-Reliability Organizations," *Journal of Public Administration Research and Theory* 1 (1991): 19–47; and H. George Frederickson and Todd LaPorte, "Airport Security, High Reliability, and the Problem of Rationality," *Public Administration Review* 62 (September 2002): 33–43.

4. Susan Stellin, "There's No Tiptoeing Past Shoe Policy," *New York Times,* July 20, 2003, sec. 5, p. 8.

5. Frederickson and LaPorte, "Airport Security, High Reliability, and the Problem of Rationality," 41.

6. *Columbia* Accident Investigation Board, *Report: Volume 1* (Washington, D.C.: U.S. Government Printing Office, 2003).

7. David Ropeik and George Gray, *Risk: A Practical Guide for Deciding What's Really Safe and What's Really Dangerous in the World around You* (New York: Mariner Books, 2002).

8. Paul Slovic and Elike U. Weber, "Perception of Risk Posed by Extreme Events" (paper prepared for the conference "Risk Management Strategies in an Uncertain World," Palisades, N.Y., April 12–13, 2002), www.ldeo.columbia.edu/CHRR/Roundtable/slovic_wp.pdf.

9. See www.biz.uiowa.edu/iem/markets/.

10. MSNBC News, "Pentagon Kills 'Terror Futures Market,'" July 29, 2003, www.msnbc.com/news/945269.asp.

11. Jan Glidewell, "Terrorism Shield Takes on New Hue," *St. Petersburg Times*, March 15, 2002, www.sptimes.com/2002/03/15/news_pf/Columns/Terrorism_shield_take.shtml.

12. Jay Leno, quoted at "Political Humor with Daniel Kurtzman," http://politicalhumor.about.com/library/blterrorhumor.htm.

13. *Borowitzreport.com*, "Cheney Admits Vast Holdings in Duct Tape and Plastic Sheeting," www.borowitzreport.com/archive_rpt.asp?rec=512.

14. William O'Rourke, "Duct Tape Dept. Good for Laughs Only," *Chicago Sun-Times*, March 4, 2003, www.suntimes.com/output/orourke/cst-edt-rour041.html.

15. Linda Hales, "This Year's Gridiron Dinner: Funny, but Not Ha-Ha Funny," *Washington Post*, March 10, 2003, C1.

16. Elisabeth Bumiller, "In Case of Emergency, Cupboards May Be Bare," *New York Times*, February 17, 2003, A9.

17. Matthew Engel, "The Terror of Duct Tape," *[London] Guardian*, February 18, 2003, 17.

18. John Tierney, "Ridge Gets the Joke, but He Hasn't Lost His Focus," *New York Times*, March 17, 2003.

19. Shawn Reese, "Homeland Security Advisory System: Possible Issues for Congressional Oversight" (Washington, D.C.: Congressional Research Service, August 6, 2003), Report RL32023, 8; and Shawn Reese, "Federal Emergency Warning Systems: An Overview" (Washington, D.C.: Congressional Research Service, January 2, 2003), Report RS21377.

20. CNN.com, "U.S, U.K. Discuss United Anti-terrorism Front," April 3, 2003, www.cnn.com/2003/US/04/03/blunkett.cnna/.

21. Home Office, "Terrorism: Frequently Asked Questions," at www.homeoffice.gov.uk/terrorism/threat/faq/index.html#10.

22. Ibid.

23. Chris Strohm, "Homeland Security May Alter Threat Advisory System," *GovExec.com*, January 9, 2004, www.govexec.com/dailyfed/0104/010904cl.htm.

24. Jennifer Barrett, "Newsweek Poll: Bin Laden to Blame for Anthrax," October 20, 2001, www.msnbc.com/news/645354.asp.

25. Harris Poll #46, "Special 9/11 Poll," September 10, 2002, www.harrisinteractive.com/harris_poll/index.asp?PID=325.

26. Robert C. Tucker, *Politics as Leadership* (Columbia: University of Missouri Press, 1981), 18–19.

27. Judith Miller, Jeff Gerth, and Don Van Natta Jr., "Planning for Terror but Failing to Act," *New York Times*, December 30, 2001.

Chapter 6

1. House Permanent Select Committee on Intelligence and Senate Select Committee on Intelligence, *Report of the Joint Inquiry into the Terrorist Attacks of September 11, 2001*, Senate Report 107-351, House Report 107-792, 107th Cong., 2d sess.

2. Ibid., xv.

3. Thomas Farragher and Alice Dembner, "America Prepares Law and Politics," *Boston Globe*, September 30, 2001, A1.

4. Peter Slevin and Mary Beth Sheridan, "Suspects Entered U.S. on Legal Visas; Men Blended In; Officials Say 49 Have Been Detained on Immigration Violations," *Washington Post*, September 18, 2001.

5. Farragher and Dembner, "America Prepares Law and Politics."

6. Martin Wolf, "Guarding the Home Front," *[London] Financial Times*, September 17, 2001, 24.

7. Farragher and Dembner, "America Prepares Law and Politics."

8. Robert O'Harrow Jr., "Six Weeks in Autumn," *Washington Post*, October 27, 2002, W6.

9. Philip Shenon, "Ashcroft Wants Quick Action on Broader Wiretapping Plan," *New York Times*, September 18, 2001.

10. Ibid.

11. Philip Shenon and Robin Toner, "U.S. Widens Policy on Detaining Suspects," *New York Times*, September 19, 2001, sec. B, p. 4.

12. American Civil Liberties Union, "In Defense of Freedom at a Time of Crisis," September 20, 2001, www.aclu.org/NationalSecurity/NationalSecurity.cfm?ID=9137&c=111.

13. Remarks by the President at Signing of the Patriot Act, Anti-Terrorism Legislation, October 25, 2001, www.whitehouse.gov/news/releases/2001/10/20011026-5.html.

14. Charles Doyle, "The USA Patriot Act: A Sketch," Congressional Research Service, April 18, 2002, www.fas.org/irp/crs/RS21203.pdf.

15. Michael R. Zimmerman, "Ashcroft Stumps for Patriot Act in Boston," *Eweek*, September 10, 2003, www.eweek.com/article2/0,4149,1259935,00.asp.

16. George W. Bush, "Address to a Joint Session of Congress and the American People," September 20, 2001, www.whitehouse.gov/news/releases/2001/09/20010920-8.html.

17. Human Rights Watch, "September 11: One Year On," September 9, 2002, www.hrw.org/press/2002/09/sept11.htm.

18. Dana Priest and Barton Gellman, "U.S. Decries but Defends Interrogations," *Washington Post*, December 26, 2002, A1.

19. Ibid.

20. Dean Schabner, "Northern Revolt: Alaska Passes Anti–Patriot Act Resolution," May 23, 2003, http://abcnews.go.com/sections/us/DailyNews/alaska_patriot030523.html.

21. Robert A. Levy, "The USA Patriot Act: We Deserve Better" (Washington, D.C.: Cato Institute), www.cato.org/current/terrorism/pubs/levy-martial-law.html.

22. "CCR Files Constitutional Challenge to Patriot Act" (2003), www.ccr-ny.org/v2/reports/report.asp?ObjID=FjMAeaTxLu&Content=278.

23. American Library Association, "Resolution on the USA Patriot Act and Related Measures that Infringe on the Rights on Library Users," January 29, 2003, www.ala.org/Content/NavigationMenu/Our_Association/Offices/ALA_Washington/Issues2/Civil_Liberties,_Intellectual_Freedom,_Privacy/The_USA_Patriot_Act_and_Libraries/ALA_Resolution_on_PATRIOT_Act.htm.

24. Eric Lichtblau, "Ashcroft Mocks Librarians and Others Who Oppose Parts of Counterterrorism Law," *New York Times*, September 16, 2003, A23.

25. Eric Lichtblau, "Government Says It Has Yet to Use New Power to Check Library Records," *New York Times*, September 19, 2003, A16.

26. Richard B. Schmitt, "Planned Sequel to Patriot Act Losing Audience," *Los Angeles Times*, July 29, 2003, part 1, p. 14.

27. Philip Shenon, "Report on USA Patriot Act Alleges Civil Rights Violations," *New York Times*, July 21, 2003, A1.

28. Dana Blanton, "Americans Say Saudis Should Do More to Fight Terror," August 1, 2003, www.foxnews.net/story/0,2933,93549,00.html.

29. Will Lester, "Poll: Freedoms a Concern," *Wisconsin State Journal*, September 11, 2003, A3.

30. Dahlia Lithwick and Julia Turner, "A Guide to the Patriot Act, Part 1," September 8, 2003, http://slate.msn.com/id/2087984.

31. Quoted by Attorney General John Ashcroft, Speech (April 2, 2003), at www.usdoj.gov/ag/speeches/2003/040203agremarks.htm.

32. U.S. Department of Justice, "Preserving Life and Liberty" (2003), www.lifeandliberty.gov/.

33. Ibid.

34. Dana Milbank, "President Asks for Expanded Patriot Act," *Washington Post*, September 11, 2003, A1.

35. David E. Sanger, "President Urging Wider U.S. Powers in Terrorism Law," *New York Times*, September 11, 2003, A1.

36. Milbank, "President Asks for Expanded Patriot Act."

37. Eric Lichtblau, "Counterterror Proposals Are a Hard Sell," *New York Times*, September 11, 2003, A19.

38. CNN.com, "Homesick Man Who Flew as Cargo Recounts Journey," September 10, 2003, www.cnn.com/2003/US/Southwest/09/10/stowaway.flight.ap/index.html.

39. Patty Davis and Beth Lewandowski, "Airport Screeners Find Loaded Gun in Teddy Bear," July 17, 2003, www.cnn.com/2003/TRAVEL/07/17/gun.teddy.bear/.

40. Jim Puzzanghera, "California Law on Driver's Licenses Spurs National Security Concerns," *SunHerald.com*, September 9, 2003, www.sunherald.com/mld/sunherald/news/politics/6731576.htm.

41. U.S. General Accounting Office, Statement of Robert J. Cramer before the Senate Committee on Finance, *Security: Counterfeit Identification and Identification Fraud Raise Security Concerns*, GAO-03-1147T, September 9, 2003.

42. *CBS Evening News*, "Airport Security Lax at Back Door," September 8, 2003, www.cbsnews.com/stories/2003/09/08/eveningnews/main572208.shtml.

43. Sara Kehaulani Goo, "Fliers to Be Rated for Risk Level," *Washington Post*, September 9, 2003, A1.

44. "Man Sneaked aboard Commuter Plane," *Holland [Michigan] Sentinel Online*, May 29, 2003, www.hollandsentinel.com/stories/052903/new_052903034.shtml; and "Airport Has No Answers for Security Breach," *ThePittsburghChannel.com*, May 28, 2003, www.thepittsburghchannel.com/news/2232715/detail.html.

45. Philip Shenon, "Airline Gave Defense Firm Passenger Files," *New York Times*, September 20, 2003, A1.

46. Stuart Taylor Jr., "Rights, Liberties, and Security: Recalibrating the Balance after September 11," *Brookings Review* 21 (Winter 2003): 25–31.

Chapter 7

1. John F. Kingdon, *Agendas, Alternatives, and Public Policies*, 2d ed. (New York: Longman, 1995), 166.

2. Robert Kupperman, Center for Strategic and International Studies, testimony before a hearing of the Committee on Governmental Affairs, United States Senate, *Federal News Service*, September 11, 1989.

3. David A. Rochefort and Roger W. Cobb, "Problem Definition: An Emerging Perspective," in *The Politics of Problem Definition: Shaping the Policy Agenda*, ed. David A. Rochefort and Robert W. Cobb (Lawrence: University of Kansas Press, 1994), 1–31.

4. Christopher J. Bosso, "The Contextual Bases of Problem Definition," in Rochefort and Cobb, *The Politics of Problem Definition*, 198–199.

5. Office of the Inspector General, U.S. Department of Justice, "The Federal Bureau of Investigation's Efforts to Improve the Sharing of Intelligence and Other Information," Audit Report 04-10, December 2003.

6. See Niles Eldredge and Stephen Jay Gould, "Punctuated Equilibria: An Alternative to Phyletic Gradualism," in *Models in Paleobiology*, ed. Thomas J. M. Schopf (San Francisco: Freeman, Cooper, 1972), 82–115.

7. Gould, *Dinosaur in a Haystack*, 136.

8. Frank R. Baumgartner and Bryan D. Jones, *Agendas and Instability in American Politics* (Chicago: University of Chicago Press, 1993), 20–21.

9. Ibid, 236.

10. Charles E. Lindblom, "The Science of 'Muddling Through,'" *Public Administration Review* 19 (1959): 79–88.

11. Aaron Wildavsky and Naomi Caiden, *The New Politics of the Budgetary Process*, 5th ed. (New York: Longman, 2004).

12. Robert Block, "FEMA Points to Flaws, Flubs in Terror Drill," *Wall Street Journal*, October 31, 2003. Excerpts from the government report come from this article. The federal agency, FEMA, did not release the report, and the reporter relied on a leaked copy. In fact, this muddy trail further underlined the difficulty of getting good information about the nation's preparedness.

13. Democratic Task Force on Homeland Security, "Federal Homeland Security Assistance to America's Hometowns: A Survey and Report from the Democratic Task Force on Homeland Security," October 29, 2003, www.house.gov/maloney/issues/Homeland/Survey.pdf.

14. Norman J. Ornstein, "Perspectives on House Reform of Homeland Security," testimony before the Subcommittee on Rules, Select Committee on Homeland Security, U.S. House of Representatives, May 19, 2003, at www.aei.org/news/newsID. 17514/news_detail.asp.

15. Theda Skocpol, *Protecting Soldiers and Mothers: The Political Origins of Social Policy in the United States* (Cambridge: Harvard University Press, 1992), 58.

16. William New, "Law Enforcement Official Says Threat Center Could Be Permanent," *GovExec.com*, September 23, 2003, www.govexec.com/dailyfed/0903/092303td1.htm.

17. Progressive Policy Institute, *America at Risk: A Homeland Security Report Card* (Washington, D.C.: Progressive Policy Institute, 2003), www.ppionline.org/ppi_ci.cfm?knlgAreaID=124&subsecid=900019&contentid=251895.

18. "Advisory Panel to Assess Domestic Response Capabilities for Terrorism Involving Weapons of Mass Distruction," *Forging America's New Normalcy: Securing Our Homeland, Protecting Our Liberty* (Santa Monica, Calif.: RAND Corp., December 2003), 2, www.rand.org/nsrd/terrpanel/volume_v/volume_v.pdf.

19. John E. Chubb and Paul E. Peterson, eds., *Can the Government Govern?* (Washington, D.C.: Brookings Institution Press, 1989).

Index

About the Author

Donald F. Kettl is professor of public affairs and political science at the Robert M. La Follette School of Public Affairs at the University of Wisconsin–Madison. He is also nonresident senior fellow at the Brookings Institution in Washington, D.C., executive director of the Century Foundation's Project on Federalism and Homeland Security, and academic coordinator of the Government Performance Project, a multiyear effort financed by the Pew Charitable Trusts to assess the performance of the American states. He is the author of numerous books, including *Team Bush: Leadership Lessons from the Bush White House; Deficit Politics: The Search for Balance in American Politics; The Transformation of Governance: Public Administration for Twenty-First Century America; Leadership at the Fed;* and *The Next Government of the United States* (forthcoming). He is the series editor for CQ Press's Public Affairs and Policy Administration Series. Professor Kettl has consulted broadly for government organizations and is a regular columnist for *Governing* magazine.